NAVAL WINGS

Royal Naval carrier-borne aircraft since 1916

Adrian Vicary

 Patrick Stephens, Cambridge

First published in 1984

Frontispiece *A standard Fairey Firefly Mk 1 fleet fighter* (Fairey).

Front endpaper *Fairey Swordfish II* HS158 *in wartime camouflage and intended for operation in an anti-submarine role from an escort carrier* (British Aerospace).

Rear endpaper *Showing the 'normal' and 'Falklands' colour schemes to advantage are the first development Sea Harrier,* XZ438 *(foreground), and* ZA176 *of 809 Squadron which shot down one Argentine Mirage III* (British Aerospace).

ISBN 0-85059-660-2

Photoset in 10 on 10 pt Baskerville by Manuset Limited, Baldock Herts. Printed in Great Britain on 115 gsm Fineblade coated cartridge, and bound, by The Garden City Press, Letchworth, Herts, for the publishers, Patrick Stephens Limited, Bar Hill, Cambridge, CB3 8EL, England.

Contents

Introduction   6

The Aircraft
Sopwith Pup and Beardmore
WB III   9
Sopwith 1 ½ -strutter   11
Sopwith 2F 1 Camel   12
Sopwith Cuckoo and
Grain Griffin   14
Parnall Panther   15
Nieuport Nightjar   15
Supermarine Seagull II   16
Blackburn Dart   17
Avro Bison   18
Blackburn Blackburn   19
Fairey IIID   19
Fairey Flycatcher   20
Fairey IIIF   22
Blackburn Ripon and
Baffin   25
Hawker Osprey   26

Hawker Nimrod   27
Fairey Seal   28
Blackburn Shark   29
Fairey Swordfish   30
Blackburn Skua   33
Gloster Sea Gladiator   34
Fairey Fulmar   35
Fairey Albacore   37
Hawker Sea Hurricane   38
Grumman Wildcat   40
Supermarine Seafire   42
Fairey Barracuda   47
Grumman Avenger   49
Vought Corsair   51
Grumman Hellcat   53
Fairey Firefly   57
Blackburn Firebrand   62
de Havilland Sea Hornet   64
Hawker Sea Fury   67
Supermarine Attacker   69
Douglas Skyraider   71

Westland Wyvern   72
Hawker Sea Hawk   76
de Havilland Sea Venom   79
Fairey Gannet   81
Supermarine Scimitar   84
Westland Whirlwind   86
de Havilland Sea Vixen   89
Westland Wessex   91
Blackburn Buccaneer   93
McDonnell Phantom   96
Westland Sea King   98
British Aerospace Sea
Harrier   100

Appendix
A summary of the main
aircraft carrier allocations of
flights and squadrons   103

Select bibliography   108
Index   109

Introduction

The aerial element of the Royal Navy, throughout its 70 years of existence, has had an almost non-stop battle for survival. Yet time and again proof has been given of its value, the most recent example obviously being the Falklands' conflict in the spring of 1982.

The Admiralty's tendency to view newfangled machinery with suspicion had an effect on the introduction of both the submarine and the aeroplane to naval service. In the case of the latter it was through the generosity of a patriotic civilian and member of the Royal Aero Club, Mr Francis McClean, that the first flying training for naval officers was started when he offered the use of two of his Short biplanes. In March 1911 the first four officers began training at the Royal Aero Club airfield at Eastchurch.

Meanwhile, on the other side of the Atlantic, another civilian flyer, Eugene Ely, was introducing the aeroplane to the United States Navy, beginning with a flight from a platform built over the foredeck of the cruiser *Birmingham* on November 14 1910. Two months later Ely made the first deck landing on the cruiser *Pennsylvania*. These events may well have had a significant effect on the development of British naval aviation, for work began in 1911 on the construction of a trackway on a British battleship.

Three battleships were to be fitted with an inclined trackway over the forward turret, the first to be used was that on *Africa*. Lieutenant Charles Rumney Samson, one of the four officers in the first Admiralty flying course at Eastchurch, took off from this ship anchored in the Medway on January 10 1912. This was the first officially recognised British flight from a ship's deck, though it is possible that he had already made a flight from *Africa* the previous month. The modified Short S.38 landed

Right *Royal Naval Sea Harriers fitted with Sidewinder missiles alongside RAF Harriers aboard HMS* Hermes *during the battle for the Falklands* (British Aerospace).

safely at Eastchurch. On May 9, Samson, now Acting Commander, consolidated his previous achievement by taking off from a similar trackway mounted on *Hibernia* while the ship was steaming at 15 knots in Weymouth Bay during the Royal Review of the Fleet. This was a world first. The third battleship to receive the take-off trackway was London and in July 1912 a second officer, Lieutenant C. L'Estrange Malone, succeeded in flying off with the ship steaming at 12 knots.

Less than a year later, events had taken a leap forward when a ship was allocated as headquarters vessel to the Naval Wing, Royal Flying Corps. The trackway mounted over the forward gun turret of the battleships rendered half the ships' main armament unusable, which was patently unacceptable. Therefore the old three-funnelled Highflyer class cruiser *Hermes* was allocated for conversion as, effectively, the world's first aircraft carrier. A trackway was built over *Hermes'* forecastle and a canvas hangar erected in front of her bridge. A second hangar was sited aft to take seaplanes which would be hoisted on and off the quarterdeck to operate from the water. The main use of the ramp was to allow seaplanes to take off using wheels fitted beneath their floats, these being jettisoned when the aeroplane lifted off. The seaplane would, of course, alight as usual. On July 28 1913 during that year's Naval Manoeuvres, a Caudron G.II biplane, serial number 55 took off from *Hermes* to become the first naval aircraft to fly from a ship specifically equipped to operate them. The Caudron was an amphibian with wheels mounted in the underside of the main floats.

When war broke out in August 1914, the Royal Naval Air Service (formed from the Naval Wing RFC two months earlier) had, for the time being, lost the ability to fly aircraft off the ship, having removed the trackway from *Hermes*, and was concentrating on seaplane operations for reconnaissance, which was then the chief occupation of naval aeroplanes (and for that matter military aeroplanes in general). In order to expand the availability of aircraft for fleet scouting, certain vessels were chosen from the vast number of merchant ships taken into naval service to be converted into seaplane carriers. These ships were the English Channel and Irish Sea ferries, which with their good turn of speed would be able to operate with the Fleet at sea, and the former Cunard liner *Campania* a holder of the Blue Riband for the fastest Atlantic crossing during the 1890s. Their main aircraft complement was necessarily seaplanes and each ship was fitted out with a hangar and workshop facilities to care for their charges. However, two of the ferries, *Ben-my-Chree* and *Vindex*, and the *Campania* were fitted with flying decks forward and from these would be taken the first 'steps' on the path of carrier pioneering carried out by the Royal Navy.

To begin with, flights were made with float-equipped aircraft using the jettisonable wheels technique; after an attempt by one of *Ben-my-Chree*'s Sopwith Schneiders had to be aborted because of engine problems, the first successful take-off was made by Flight Lieutenant W. L. Welsh in Schneider number *1559* from *Campania* on August 6 1915. Three months later, *Vindex* was the platform for the first flight of a landplane—ie, an aeroplane with a wheel and tailskid undercarriage and no means of support in the event of a watery landing. For the purposes of this book, the date of November 3 1915, when Flight Lieutenant Fowler flew Bristol Scout C, number *1255*, off *Vindex*'s flying deck marks the dawn of the dedicated carrier-borne aircraft. Admittedly the Scout had to fly back to its home base at Eastchurch to land but a big step forward had been taken. The problem remained as to how to bring the aircraft in to land on the ship herself.

The Aircraft

Sopwith Pup and Beardmore WB III

The origins of the Pup lie in the one-off single-seater reputedly built from full size drawings done in chalk on the floor of the Sopwith experimental shop by Harry Hawker, the firm's chief test pilot, in the autumn of 1915. It was known as 'Hawker's Runabout' owing to his use of it as a personal transport and aerobatic machine. The prototype Pup, serial *3691*, completed early in 1916, was in the hands of the Central Flying School by March for evaluation. The aircraft was soon ordered into quantity production for both the RNAS and the RFC. Pre-production Pup number *9496* was accepted into service in July 1916 and allocated to No 3 Wing RNAS in France. To the Royal Naval Air Service the type was known as the Sopwith 9901 after the serial number of the first production aircraft built by William Beardmore & Co Ltd.

The Pup was first taken up for use at sea as a Zeppelin fighter of greater capability than the currently used Sopwith Baby floatplane, which was not liked owing to difficulty in handling on the water and the need to hoist it out from the parent ship. Flight Commander F. J. Rutland of the *Manxman* (ex-Midland Railway Isle of Man steamer) was instrumental in obtaining the Pup, arguing the case for interception of Zeppelins at altitude—procurement was also favoured in the report of the Grand Fleet Committee on Air Requirements of February 5 1917. Rutland developed take-off on *Manxman* to the point where the wheels were off the deck in a run of under 20 ft. The agility of the aircraft made this possible. Further trials on a special deck built on *Manxman*'s flying deck led to the use of the type in light cruisers, starting with the *Yarmouth*. The take-off run was brought down to an incredible 14 ft 9 ins. A successful attack was made on Zeppelin *L.23* on August 21 1917 by Flight Sub-Lieutenant B. A. Smart flying from the platform on *Yarmouth*. The

Ship's Pup, a Beardmore-built Sopwith Pup with normal wheels for ramp take-off from battleships, battle cruisers and cruisers (Bruce Robertson).

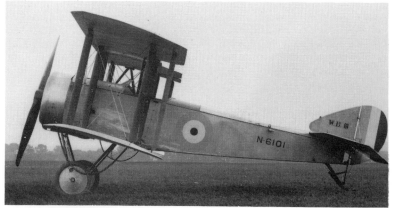

Left *Beardmore WB III, a shipborne version of the Sopwith Pup. This example is of the Admiralty SB 3F (Shipborne Type 3 with folding undercarriage) type as opposed to the SB 3D type with dropping (jettisonable) undercarriage* (Bruce Robertson).

Left *A Beardmore-built Sopwith Pup (Admiralty Type 9901A) with skid undercarriage on trials with a dummy deck* (Bruce Robertson).

pilot had to ditch his Pup near to a destroyer and was picked up by one of her boats. His aircraft was lost. The successful use of the platform was taken a step further, again by Rutland, when he made trial flights from platforms erected on 'B' & 'Y' turrets of the battlecruiser *Repulse* in October 1917. These could be trained as necessary without the ship having to alter course into wind. Though this enabled capital ships to fly off aircraft for scouting and interception of hostile aircraft it did nothing to solve the problem of bringing down the aircraft on board ship when out of range of a land base.

Trials to find a suitable method of deck-landing aircraft began as early as the end of 1915 at the Experimental Construction Depot at the Isle of Grain. In 1917, a 210 ft diameter dummy deck was constructed at Port Victoria to try out various methods of arresting aircraft and the trials made involved the use of several Sopwith Pups with both wheel and skid undercarriages. There still remained the problem of the lack of a suitable sea-going deck for a landing attempt until July 1917 when the *Furious* joined the Fleet. She had been building as a fast cruiser armed with two 18 in guns in single mountings, one forward and one aft. The decision was taken before completion to abandon the fore turret and remodel the foredeck to accept a 228 ft flying deck with hangar space under the after end and forward of the bridge structure.

Almost immediately things started happening. In

Scapa Flow on August 2 1917 Squadron Commander E. H. Dunning, flying Pup *N6453*, brought his machine along the port side of the ship which was steaming at 26 knots into a 21-knot wind giving a wind over the deck of some 47 knots. As he came forward of *Furious'* superstructure he gently side-slipped the Pup inboard until he was floating over the flight deck where his fellow officers were waiting to grab the aircraft as it touched down. Crude perhaps but effective; the world's first landing by aeroplane on a moving ship. A second successful landing was made on August 7, though Dunning's Pup suffered slight damage to its elevators when it was blown back against the hangar hatch coaming. Undaunted, this brave pilot took over a second Pup and took off for another attempt. Sadly, tragedy was waiting. Unhappy with his position over the deck, he opened up the engine to make a second circuit only for the engine to falter, causing the aircraft to stall. Although the Pup was still over the deck, the impact caused the aircraft to bounce over the starboard side of the ship and fall into the sea. Dunning was apparently knocked unconscious and was unable to escape from the cockpit, which was submerged.

Rutland was appointed to succeed Dunning and made a deck landing himself but was convinced that a full-length unobstructed deck was necessary for practicality. As it was impossible to withdraw *Furious* from service for the length of time needed to rebuild her upperworks, a compromise was attempted in which a second flying deck was built aft of the funnel 300 ft in length and eliminating the second 18 in gun. The ship was back in service in March 1918 after five months in dockyard hands and trials began in deck-landing aircraft with skid undercarriages using the longitudinal arrester cables fitted on the new deck. Should the aircraft fail to be stopped, they would be prevented from crashing into the ship's superstructure by a suspended rope barrier carried by a gantry aft of the funnel. However, the major drawback of this arrangement was that the air turbulence caused by the ship's upperworks, aggravated by the hot gases emitting from the funnel, made it extremely difficult to get the nimble Pup down positively and several narrow escapes occurred when aircraft fell over the side of the deck.

It was early recognised that aircraft stowed onboard ship, especially with the limited hangar space available in the early carriers, took up a great deal of room and thereby limited the number of machines that could be stowed. It would have been possible to carry some in a dismantled state but that would have needed extra time spent on reassembly for use. Some thought on this problem led to the development of a variant of the Pup, work on which was to be carried out by Beardmore. Under the designation WB III, the major reworking of the design resulted in an aircraft bearing no family resemblance. By eliminating wing stagger, the mainplanes could be folded back by means of a hinge on the rear spar to lie parallel with the fuselage, which was lengthened to allow clearance at the tailplane. The prototype WB III was the last aircraft from Beardmore's first Pup production batch, number *9950*. Naval acceptance of the design led to an order for 100 production machines. These were of two sub-types—officially designated the SB 3F and SB 3D. In the former, the F suffix indicated a folding undercarriage and in the latter D covered a dropping (jettisonable) undercarriage. In both cases, the S.B. indicated Sopwith-Beardmore in recognition of the type's origins. The WB III proved less handy than its forebear and had an undistingished service career.

Sopwith Pup: *Span* 26 ft 6 in; *Length* 19 ft 3¾ in; *Height* 9 ft 5 in; *Wing area* 254 sq ft; *Engine* One 80 hp Le Rhone 9C rotary; *All up weight* 1,225 lb; *Maximum speed* 115 mph at sea level; *Service ceiling* 17,500 ft; *Endurance* 3 hours; *Armament* 1 × 0.303 in Lewis machine-gun.

Beardmore WB III: *Span* 25 ft 0 in; *Length* 20 ft 2½ in; *Height* 8 ft 1¼ in: *Wing area* 243 sq ft; *Engine* One 80 hp Le Rhone 9C, or 80 hp Clerget rotary; *All up weight* 1,289 lb; *Maximum speed* 103 mph at sea level; *Service ceiling* 12,400 ft; *Endurance* 2.75 hours; *Armament* 1 × 0.303 in Lewis machine-gun.

Sopwith 1½-strutter

The 1½-strutter was something of a multi-role combat aircraft and gave valuable service with both Royal Flying Corps and Royal Naval Air Service units in France in the role of long-range bomber, bomber escort and reconnaissance machine. In the Home Defence role the type served with several squadrons based around London to help defend the capital against the Gotha and Zeppelin bombers, usually in company with a motley collection of types such as BE 12s, RE 8s and Camels.

However, the role with which this account is concerned is that of pioneer deck-flying aircraft. The primary role of most operational ship-borne aircraft during the First World War was reconnaissance, seeking out enemy ships or shore positions and directing fall of shot from capital ships' main armament. To this end, the 1½-strutter, or Ship's Strutter, was operated from turret platforms in the big ships, the first successful flight being made from

A Sopwith Ship Strutter, the navalised version of the 1½-strutter, seen engaging in the longitudinal arresting wires on landing on HMS Argus (Bruce Robertson).

the battlecruiser HMAS *Australia* on April 4 1918. Ship's Strutters were operated in both two-seat and single-seat versions as with their land-based counterparts and in RNAS service were designated Type 9400 and Type 9700 respectively. Trials were carried out in *Argus* and *Vindex* and the type was involved in the deck landing trials carried out in *Furious* after her second flight deck had been constructed. Both wheel and skid undercarriages were used and flotation equipment was installed to keep the aircraft afloat in the event of ditching being necessary. At first the inflatable flotation bags were fitted either side of the forward fuselage ahead of the wings but later they were relocated within the rear fuselage. Defensive armament in ship-borne service was a standard Lewis gun on a ring mounting in the rear cockpit, though it was sometimes unshipped to save weight. The forward-firing, pilot-operated, Vickers gun was omitted from naval aircraft for the same reason, this weight saving allowing wireless equipment to be carried.

Sopwith 1½-strutter (Ship's Strutter): *Span* 33 ft 6 in; *Length* 25 ft 3 in; *Height* 10 ft 3 in; *Wing area* 346 sq ft; *Engine* One 110 hp Clerget 9Z rotary (some had 130 hp Clerget); *All up weight* 2,149 lb; *Maximum speed* 106 mph at sea level; *Service ceiling* 15,000 ft; *Endurance* 3.75 hours; *Armament* 1 × 0.303 in Lewis machine-gun on ring mount in aft cockpit.

Sopwith 2F 1 Camel

The 2F 1, or Ship's Camel, was a devotedly naval variant of the Sopwith F 1 Camel which operated widely with the Royal Flying Corps and Royal Naval Air Service from the summer of 1917 to the end of the war, building up a reputation akin to that of the Spitfire in the second great conflict. Flying in prototype form in March 1917, the chief role for the 2F.1 was to be in anti-Zeppelin operations from seaplane carriers and other vessels' turret platforms. It was more or less a foregone conclusion that the Camels flown in anger in such a way would have to ditch in the sea at the end of their missions as they were likely to be out of range of friendly land bases on such occasions and deck-landing trials were still land-based at that time.

Despite this drawback, two events were to prove the worth of this bold risk in the last few months of the Great War. The first occurred on July 19 1918. Eight Ship's Camels were embarked in *Furious* with the intention of making an attack on the naval airship station at Tondern in Schleswig-Holstein. Flown from the ship at dawn from a position northwest of the target, seven Camels set off on the 80-mile journey, each with a load of two 50 lb bombs. One aircraft was forced to ditch due to engine trouble on the way in but the others, in two waves of three, reached Tondern 1 hour and 20 minutes after take off. Surprise was complete and the pilots' aim accurate. Bombs fell on the huge shed containing Zeppelins *L.54* and *L.60*, penetrating the roof and igniting the airships' highly inflammable contents. Also destroyed was a small observation balloon.

The raid was an obvious success but the aftermath for the Camels and their pilots was not touched with such fortune. Two pilots managed to regain the friendly ships, ditching and being picked up by a destroyer but the other four were not so lucky. Short of fuel, three force-landed in Denmark and were interned and the fourth pilot was drowned when he ditched out of range of rescue. Despite the sombre ending, the operation gave ample proof of the efficacy of a ship-borne strike on a land target and could only strengthen the desire to perfect the technique of recovering the aircraft 'dry' aboard ship.

The second event was on August 11 1918, this time a solo effort. More pioneering work by Charles Samson, now a Colonel in the Royal Air Force, had produced a converted towed lighter (the original purpose of which was to carry flying boats with a striking force to increase their effective range) from which a Sopwith Camel could fly. Fitted with a flying platform, a mini flight deck about 40 ft long, the lighter would be towed by a destroyer at top speed, enabling the Camel, with its engine at full power, to lift off with the shortest of runs.

On the day in question, elements of the Harwich Force were in the Heligoland Bight on an offensive sweep when a Zeppelin was seen in the vicinity at high altitude. Flying boats with the force were unable to intercept so the lighter-borne Camel, *N6812* under tow of the destroyer *Redoubt*, was launched. Lieutenant Stuart Culley, a Canadian, was in the cockpit. More than half an hour was required to draw near the Zeppelin and even then

Culley was still beneath the airship. With the Camel at extreme altitude, desperate measures were needed, so pulling back the stick and pointing the aeroplane at the underside of his adversary, Culley opened fire with his two machine-guns. The Camel quickly fell away in the stall but the damage had been done, *L.53* was on fire and falling. The Camel was successfully ditched and both pilot and machine recovered, the aeroplane surviving to this day in the Imperial War Museum.

With the war over, the Camel's first-line service ended but the type continued in small numbers in the role of deck-landing experimenter aboard *Argus* and *Eagle* into the early 20s.

Sopwith 2F 1 Ship's Camel: *Span* 26 ft 11 in; *Length* 18 ft 8 in; *Height* 9 ft 1 in; *Wing area* 221 sq ft; *Engine* One 150 hp Bentley B.R.1 rotary; *All up weight* 1,530 lb; *Maximum speed* 124 mph at 6,500 ft; *Service ceiling* 17,300 ft; *Endurance* About 3 hours; *Armament* 1 × 0.303 in Vickers machine-gun fixed forward-firing in fuselage top decking, 1 × 0.303 in Lewis machine gun above centre section of top wing (*NB* Culley's Camel, *N6812*, had a special twin Lewis mounting above the centre section and no Vickers machine-gun), 2 × 50 lb bombs beneath lower wings.

The shipborne version of the Sopwith Camel, the Type 2F 1, differed in armament from the conventional Type 1F 1 Camels by having only a single Vickers machine-gun firing through the propeller arc, but it did have a Lewis machine-gun mounted on the top wing as exemplified in this view (Bruce Robertson).

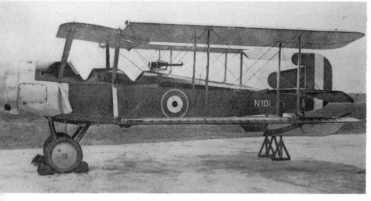

Top *The RAF's first standard torpedo bomber, the Cuckoo, designed by Sopwith but built by other firms under contract. This Blackburn-built Cuckoo is seen on torpedo-dropping training at Gosport (Bruce Robertson).* **Above** *An aircraft built by the Isle of Grain RNAS Experimental Construction Department in 1918, the Grain Griffin. The first of the seven built had a Sunbeam Arab engine but N101 shown is powered by a BR2, to judge its performance with the Panther (Bruce Robertson).*

Sopwith Cuckoo and Grain Griffin

Commodore Murray Sueter, tireless advocate and supporter of naval flying, was instrumental in encouraging Sopwith to produce a landplane torpedo carrier for the Royal Naval Air Service. The resulting aeroplane, at first known as the Sopwith T.1, was completed in prototype form in June 1917 and sent to the trials establishment at the Isle of Grain. Initial tests proved the type to be worthy of order and the first production contract was placed in August with the Scottish shipbuilding firm of Fairfield. As the prime purpose of the T.1 was to be the carrying and launching of a torpedo, it

was natural that attention should be paid to the pioneering work of the Blackburn company in designing torpedo gear for their general purpose seaplane (the Blackburn G.P. of 1916) and as events unfolded the lion's share of the production T.1s was to be built by the Yorkshire company.

With the art of aerial torpedo attack in its infancy, an unavoidably long gestation was passed before the T.1 was ready to enter service, the first unit to equip being the Torpedo Aeroplane School at East Fortune in the summer of 1918. Pilots trained by this establishment subsequently joined the newly formed No 185 Squadron RAF in October, making the first embarkation in *Argus* on October 19. Before another month had passed the Great War was over and with it the likelihood of the T.1's use against the German High Seas Fleet, which in any case had been largely subdued since the Battle of Jutland two and a half years earlier. The name Cuckoo was bestowed upon the Sopwith T.1 after the war's end, two marks being distinguished by their different engines. In the Cuckoo Mk I this was a Sunbeam Arab and in the Mk II a Wolseley Viper.

Contemporary with the T.1 was the Sopwith B.1 bomber, the sole example of which saw service alongside Airco D.H.4s with No 5 Wing RNAS based at Dunkirk. The B.1 was not intended to operate from aircraft carriers but modification of the design was undertaken by the RNAS Experimental Construction Depot at Port Victoria on the Isle of Grain, to produce a carrier-borne reconnaissance bomber. Known as the Grain Griffin, seven aircraft were built and used mainly for various trials. They were too late to see service in the war but after carrying out deck trials in *Vindictive* in October 1918, several of them were used for reconnaissance in support of White Russian forces against the Bolsheviks in 1919. After this the Griffin soon disappeared from service but the Sopwith Cuckoo stayed on until 1923, when the final examples, shore-based at Gosport, were retired.

Sopwith Cuckoo Mk I: *Span* 46 ft 9 in; *Length* 28 ft 6 in; *Height* 10 ft 8 in; *Wing area* 566 sq ft; *Engine* One 200 hp Sunbeam Arab; *All up weight* 3,883 lb; *Maximum speed* 103.5 mph at 2,000 ft; *Service ceiling* 12,100 ft; *Endurance* 4 hours; *Armament* 1 × 18 in Mk IX torpedo.

Grain Griffin: *Span* 42 ft 6 in; *Length* 27 ft 3 in; *Height* 10 ft 6 in; *Wing area* 506 sq ft; *Engine* One 200 hp Sunbeam Arab; *All up weight* 2,858 lb; *Maximum speed* 115 mph at 5,000 ft; *Service ceiling* 19,000 ft; *Endurance* 3 hours; *Armament* 1 × 0.303 in Lewis machine-gun on movable mount behind rear cockpit.

Parnall Panther

The Parnall Panther ship-borne spotter-reconnaissance aeroplane operated alongside its contemporary, the Nightjar fleet fighter, it being also the first post-war purveyor of its role. Records state that the Panther was produced to the Admiralty N.2a category, which is a little odd as that supposedly referred to light boats or seaplanes. It is possible that at the time the Parnall design was being formulated in 1917, the ability of the Panther to ditch 'safely' was seen as qualifying it for the seaplane category! The design incorporated a hydrovane forward of the wheels to prevent the aircraft tipping over on entering the water and a pair of inflatable flotation bags each side of the undercarriage struts to keep it afloat once it had ditched.

The first of six prototypes flew in 1917 and extensive trials were carried out before a production order was placed. As this happened just before the Armistice, the order was cut back from 300 to 150 to be built, not by Parnall but by the British and Colonial Aeroplane Co Ltd (later Bristol). An interesting feature of the type was its monocoque fuselage structure, the rear portion of which, for carrier stowage, could be folded to starboard on a hinge line just aft of the observer's cockpit. The two-man crew was seated high in the prominently humped fuselage, the pilot gaining his cockpit through a cut-out in the upper wing. The first Panthers came off the line in 1919 and joined No 205 Squadron RAF based at Leuchars. Aircraft would be detached as necessary to operate aboard *Argus*. The 1923 re-shuffle of units saw the formation of the Panther-equipped No 441 Flight which saw brief service in the newly completed *Hermes* in 1924 before reforming with the Fairey IIID.

Parnall Panther: *Span* 29 ft 6 in; *Length* 24 ft 11 in (14 ft 6 in folded); *Height* 10 ft 6 in; *Wing area* 336 sq ft; *Engine* One 230 hp Bentley B.R.2 rotary; *All up weight* 2,595 lb; *Maximum speed* 108 mph at 6,500 ft; *Service ceiling* 14,500 ft; *Endurance* $4\frac{1}{4}$ hours; *Armament* 1 × 0.303 in Lewis machine-gun in rear cockpit.

Nieuport Nightjar

One of the manufacturing companies which had built aircraft during the First World War was the Gloucestershire Aircraft Co of Cheltenham. In the lean early post-war years, this firm, which had built aircraft designed by other concerns during the conflict, bravely decided to set up its own design office and acquired the services of H. P. Folland,

The first of the Panthers, the aircraft used for type trials (Bruce Robertson).

chief designer of the Nieuport and General Aircraft Co when they closed down in 1920. As a development of the Nieuport Nighthawk design, the fledgling company produced the Gloucestershire Mars series, early examples of which had a moderate success in sales to the Imperial Japanese Navy. Each succeeding variant in the Mars series was given a new type number and it was the Mars X which would enter service as the Royal Navy's first post-war fighter in 1922.

Powered by a Bentley rotary engine and still carrying the old manufacturer's name as the

Nightjars, navalised version of the Nieuport Nighthawk, seen in use by No 203 Squadron on HMS Argus *during the Chanak Crisis over the Dardanelles in 1922* (Bruce Robertson).

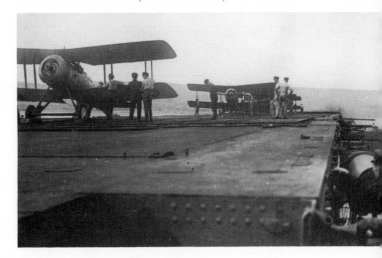

Nieuport Nightjar, the new aeroplane did not offer a great advancement over the preceeding Sopwith Camel. Nevertheless, the type saw some service in 1922 when the Leuchars-based No 203 Squadron was taken by Argus to support British forces at Chanak, caught up in the war over Turkish nationalism. Although the Nightjars did not see any action as the situation was resolved diplomatically, this event served as an early example of the value of the aircraft carrier in getting aircraft quickly to far-flung trouble spots.

The following year saw the rearrangement of the Royal Air Force's naval units, with the Nightjars being re-formed into No 401 Flight for service aboard *Argus*. For flight deck operations the aircraft were fitted with claws on their axles to engage the fore-and-aft arrestor cables. 401's Nightjars continued to serve until replaced by Flycatchers in 1924.

Nieuport Nightjar: *Span* 28 ft 0 in; *Length* 18 ft 4 in; *Height* 9 ft 0 in; *Wing area* 270 sq ft; *Engine* One 230 hp Bentley B.R.2 rotary; *All up weight* 2,165 lb; *Maximum speed* 120 mph at sea level; *Service ceiling* 19,000 ft; *Endurance* 2 hours; *Armament* 2 × 0.303 in Vickers machine-guns fixed forward-firing.

Supermarine Seagull II

Something of an oddity amongst deck-landing aircraft in Royal Navy service was the Supermarine Seagull II, coming from the long line of Supermarine amphibians designed by Reginald Mitchell. Another of these, the Sea Lion II, won the 1922 Schneider Trophy race at Naples in the hands of Henri Biard, the company's first chief test pilot. The Seagull itself was developed from the Supermarine Seal by installing a 480 hp Napier Lion II engine in place of the earlier 450 hp version. A pair

of newly built Seagull prototypes followed for trials work and then the first of three small orders was placed for production aircraft.

Their role was to be the traditional gunnery spotter-reconnaissance amalgam with a three-man crew, the pilot occupying a single cockpit forward of the wings, the observer in a cockpit in line with the trailing edges and a gunner situated at a third position a little further aft. Initial trials were made in 1922 and the next year deliveries permitted the formation of No 440 Flight, which was to serve in the aircraft carrier *Eagle*. The Seagull II was found to be of no potential naval use as a flight deck aircraft, presumably because a 'flying boat with wheels' did not offer any advantages over a landplane which could, if need be, have a float undercarriage fitted. Such a type, the Fairey IIID, replaced *Eagle*'s Seagulls early in 1925.

The building of the Seagull was, however, no waste of time. Firstly, the production batches, though small, enabled Supermarine to survive as a manufacturer in the aircraft building slump after the First World War until the revival of the mid-20s. Secondly, the continuous development of the amphibian led eventually to the famous Walrus and its successor, the Sea Otter, which numbered air-sea rescue amongst their many duties, a few operating in that role from carrier decks in later years.

Supermarine Seagull II: *Span* 46 ft 0 in; *Length* 37 ft 9 in; *Height* 14 ft 0 in; *Wing area* 593 sq ft; *Engine* One 492 hp Napier Lion IIB; *All up weight* 5,691 lb; *Maximum speed* 108 mph at sea level; *Service ceiling* 9,150 ft; *Endurance* 4½ hours; *Armament* 1 × 0.303 in Lewis machine-gun on ring mount in aft cockpit.

Supermarine Seagull II of 440 Flight based on HMS Eagle *in 1924* (Bruce Robertson).

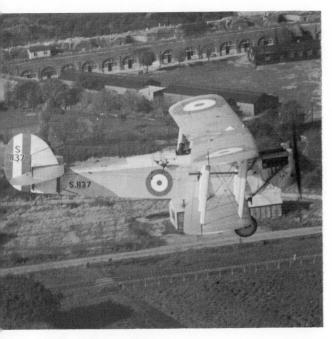

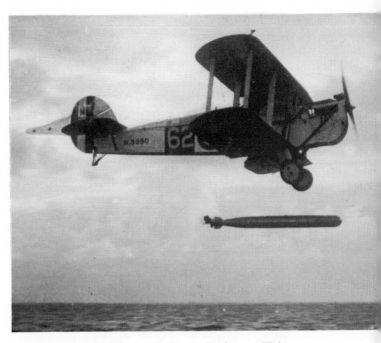

Blackburn Dart

Throughout aviation history, private venture design work has been responsible for the appearance of many important aircraft, and the Dart was one of them. After the end of the Great War, British companies which had produced thousands of aircraft during the conflict, found themselves suddenly bereft of work. It took some time for governmental authorities to sort themselves out, so it fell to the companies to look to their own salvation. In the case of Blackburn, their attention turned to the design of a single-seat biplane torpedo carrier. Under the company designation T.1, and given the name Swift, a single prototype was built during the first half of 1920 and exhibited at the Olympia Aero Show in London in July. The Air Ministry came to the decision that a replacement was needed for the Sopwith Cuckoo and bought the Swift prototype, while an order was placed for three further machines with some modification, to serve as prototypes for a definitive aeroplane. The Swift carried out trials at the A & AEE Martlesham Heath and at Gosport while work proceeded on the new machines, T.2s which were to carry the name Dart. The first of these flew initially in October 1921 and after more trials the type was ordered into production.

Deliveries commenced in March 1922 and the first operational units formed on Darts the following year. Nos 460 and 461 Flights, both based at Gosport to begin with, embarked in *Eagle* with the

Above left *Blackburn Dart of the Torpedo Development Flight, Gosport, flying over the fort at its home base in July 1928* (Bruce Robertson). **Above** *A Dart torpedo bomber in 'action', a sleeve target streaming aft.*

Mediterranean Fleet and *Furious* with the Home Fleet respectively in 1924. Three more flights were to form, one of these for *Furious* and the other two joining *Courageous* in 1928. With the Dart, the Fleet Air Arm cut its teeth in the art of aerial torpedo dropping, countless sorties being flown in mock attacks on friendly ships—all of which would stand the formation in good stead when the Swordfish put experience to the test in the next war. Apart from its chief *raison d'etre*, the Dart put a first to its credit when Flight Lieutenant Gerald Boyce deck-landed *N9804* at night on *Furious* on July 1 1926.

Replacement of the type started in 1929 when *Furious'* No 462 Flight changed to the Dart's successor from Blackburn, the Ripon. However, the two flights in *Courageous* did not relinquish their Darts until 1933, when Baffins took over and the flights merged to form 810 Squadron.

Blackburn Dart: *Span* 45 ft 5¾ in; *Length* 35 ft 4½ in; *Height* 12 ft 11 in; *Wing area* 654 sq ft; *Engine* One 450 hp Napier Lion IIB; *All up weight* 6,383 lb; *Maximum speed* 107 mph at 3,000 ft; *Service ceiling* 12,700 ft; *Range* 285 miles; *Armament* 1 × 18 in Mk VIII or IX torpedo or 1,040 lb of bombs under the wings.

Above *The ugliest of them all, the Avro Bison sea reconnaissance and fleet gunnery spotter to Specification 3/21 (Bruce Robertson).*

Left *One of the dozen Avro Bison Is, N9592, modified to Mk II standard.*

Avro Bison

A 1921 requirement for a fleet spotter-reconnaissance aeroplane brought about the design of two of the Navy's most ungainly looking types. The first of these was the Avro 555 Bison. The sheer size of the fuselage was due to a combination of two features— obtaining a good forward view for the pilot and providing a spacious cabin for the observers. As a single engine was to be used, the pilot's cockpit was sited above and behind it and the top cowling sharply raked down to the nose. To give access to the cockpit, a permanent ladder was fixed to the starboard side of the forward fuselage. The observers' cabin was totally enclosed within the fuselage but featured a large window each side. Just aft of this cabin, positioned on the top decking, was a Scarff ring mounting for a Lewis machine-gun. The first prototype Bison flew in 1921, the date now apparently unknown, and production aircraft appeared the following year. The first batch of Bisons, Mk 1s, featured the upper wing flush with the top of the fuselage but this was revised in the Mark II to be strut-mounted above it.

No 3 Squadron Royal Air Force, then part of the Coastal Area based at Gosport, took Bisons on charge in 1922 and on disbandment on April 1 1923, the unit's aircraft were distributed between four new naval flights numbered 420-423. Of these Nos 421 and 423 Flights formed on the Avro Bisons and operated with the aircraft carriers *Argus, Furious, Hermes* and *Eagle* until 1929 when the spotter-reconnaissance flights were reorganised and 421 and 423 became 447 and 448 Flights respectively. Very soon afterwards the Bisons were replaced by Fairey IIIFs.

Avro Bison Mk II: *Span* 46 ft 0 in; *Length* 36 ft 0 in; *Height* 14 ft 2 in; *Wing area* 630 sq ft; *Engine* One 480 hp Napier Lion II; *All up weight* 6,132 lb; *Maximum speed* 110 mph; *Service ceiling* 12,000 ft; *Range* 360 miles; *Armament* 1 × 0.303 in Lewis machine-gun on ring mounting and 1 × 0.303 in Vickers machine-gun fixed forward-firing.

Blackburn Blackburn

The second of the two types developed to the 1921 fleet spotter-reconnaissance requirement, the Blackburn R-1, took several construction details from that company's Dart torpedo biplane. The enormous fuselage, like that of the Avro Bison, contained the cabin for the two observers and the pilot's cockpit was again mounted high above the engine. The pilot gained his position by means of foot and hand holds built into the port side of the fuselage. The basic wing and tailplane structures of the Dart were used with little alteration, though the gap between the mainplanes was greater even though the upper wing was mounted flush with the top of the fuselage. In the Blackburn Mk II the upper wing was raised clear of the fuselage on struts, as was done with the Bison. Aft of the observers' cabin was a Scarff ring mounting for the Lewis machine-gun. The Blackburn Blackburn took to the air for the first time during 1922 and the first production Mark Is appeared the next year.

Initial deliveries were to 422 Flight at Gosport with deck trials being made aboard *Argus*, and the first commission in *Eagle* with the Mediterranean Fleet. Only one other flight formed on Blackburns, No 420, and in the 1929 renumbering these units became 450 and 449 Flights respectively. After their

spell with *Eagle*, 422 Flight served aboard *Argus*, some time being spent on the China Station, the furthest afield that the type saw duty. The Blackburn outlived the Bison, lasting until 1931 when, similarly, replacement took place with Fairey IIIFs.

Blackburn Blackburn Mk I: *Span* 45 ft 6½ in; *Length* 36 ft 2 in; *Height* 12 ft 6 in; *Wing area* 650 sq ft; *Engine* One 450 hp Napier Lion IIB; *All up weight* 5,962 lb; *Maximum speed* 122 mph at 3,000 ft; *Service ceiling* 12,950 ft; *Range* 440 miles; *Armament* 1 × 0.303 in Lewis machine-gun on ring mounting and 1 × 0.303 in Vickers machine-gun fixed forward-firing.

Fairey IIID

During the First World War, the Admiralty issued standard classifications to cover different types of aircraft, one among these being the N.2a designation for light flying boats or seaplanes. Fairey Aviation of Hayes produced a pair of prototypes (naval serials *N9* and *N10*) in this category which were to lead to the famous and prolific Fairey III series. Each of the prototypes was a seaplane equipped with twin main floats and a tail float and it was the second of these aircraft which was given the original 'III' type designation. In 1917 this aeroplane was given a wheel undercarriage and thus became the prototype for the IIIA reconnaissance aircraft which went into production. The

Blackburn Blackburn TSR (Torpedo-Spotter-Reconnaissance) aircraft of 422 Flight prior to embarking on HMS Eagle, *June 1924 (Bruce Robertson).*

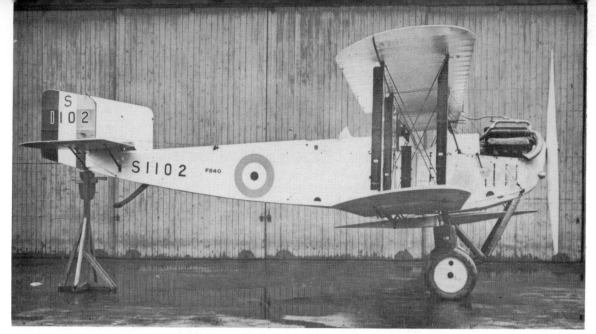

Fairey IIID (constructor's number F840), S1102.

IIIB was a reworked version for light bomber-seaplane duties. The two roles were merged in the following Fairey IIIC seaplane which appeared in service just prior to the Armistice in November 1918, though the type was to see a brief period of active service with the North Russian Expeditionary Force in 1919.

In August 1920, the test pilot Colonel Vincent Nicholl made the first flight of the IIIC (Improved) which was the prototype of the IIID to specification 38/22. This aircraft was also fitted with floats, though the type was destined to operate with either float or wheel undercarriages as required. Powerplant varied from batch to batch between the Rolls-Royce Eagle VIII and Napier Lion series, though the latter eventually became standard. Extensive trials were carried out aboard *Argus* in 1922 with particular attention to the ship's arrester gear, which at that time was of the fore-and-aft cable type. The IIID was prone to landing accidents using that arrangement with the result that deck-landings were made without arrestor hooks when the type entered service. Deck trials were also made with float-equipped IIIDs using wheeled dollys for take-off.

Introduction to naval service began in 1924, the year of formation of the Fleet Air Arm of the RAF. The first unit to form on the Fairey IIID was No 441 Flight which had been operating Parnall Panthers, shore-based at Leuchars. No 441 embarked in the carrier *Hermes* and after a spell in the Mediterranean left for the China Station in 1925. Also in the Far East, No 444 Flight operated from the cruiser *Vindictive* with IIID seaplanes. Six

flights operated IIIDs in the period 1924 to 1930, though machines allocated varied in number from flight to flight. For example, No 445 Flight operated the odd 'D' alongside its principal equipment of Fairey IIIFs in *Courageous* during 1929. The latter type began to succeed the IIID in 1927.

Fairey IIID: *Span* 46 ft 1 in (13 ft 0 in folded); *Length* 31 ft 5 in; *Height* 12 ft 0 in; *Wing area* 474 sq ft; *Engine* One 375 hp Rolls-Royce Eagle VIII; *All up weight* 4,918 lb; *Maximum speed* 106 mph; *Service ceiling* 17,000 ft; *Range* 550 miles; *Armament* 1 × 0.303 in Vickers machine-gun fixed forward-firing and 1 × 0.303 in Lewis machine-gun on ring mount in aft cockpit.

Fairey Flycatcher

The Flycatcher was the Fleet Air Arm's premier fighter of the inter-war years, highly praised by its pilots for its outstanding performance and manoeuvrability. The type was designed to specification 6/22 for a single-seat shipboard fighter and was in competition with a design from Parnall called the Plover. The latter aeroplane was found to be inferior to the Flycatcher and, although a small

Right *Fleet fighter of the '20s, the Fairey Flycatcher. Example shown in flying during 1931 near Leuchars where the RAF Base had accommodation for five fleet flights disembarked from carriers* (Bruce Robertson).

quantity was built, they were quickly withdrawn from service when sufficient examples of the Fairey machine became available. Three Flycatcher prototypes were ordered, each to be fitted with a different undercarriage (landplane, float and amphibian) for trials.

The landplane prototype, *N163*, was first into the air when Vincent Nicholl took it up from Hamble on November 28 1922. Service trials at Martlesham Heath gave a clear indication of the Flycatcher's promise, especially favoured being the excellent characteristics for deck-landing of a fine field of vision from the cockpit and a remarkably short landing run, due to the very low stalling speed (below 50 mph) and the full-width wide chord flaps. These flaps were referred to as the 'Fairey patent camber-changing gear'. Carrier deck trials were started in February 1923 aboard *Argus*. To begin with, the aircraft was fitted with axle-mounted arrestor claws to engage the then favoured fore-and-aft wires and these were fitted in production aircraft till 1926 when the system was finally abandoned. From that time landings were made 'free' and though transverse arrestor cables appeared in 1931, the Flycatcher happily completed its service career without any such assistance.

Naturally this nimble little fighter served in all the fleet's aircraft carriers, starting in 1924 with 402 Flight aboard *Eagle*, the unit having formed ashore the previous year at Leuchars. The strength built up to a total of eight flights embarked by 1930. Of these, the flights embarked in *Furious, Courageous* and *Glorious* had the thrill of operating as slip flights from the ships' forward hangars. These hangars opened directly on to the forecastle deck which formed a runway tapering to the bow, below the level of the main flight deck. The Flycatchers would be restrained at the back of the hangar while their engines were run up to full power and then released to roar out of the hangar and away. For more than ten years the Flycatcher served as the FAA's sole fighter type, not only in the fleet carriers but as turret platform fighters in battleships and as float-planes from the catapults of other ships.

Development of a Flycatcher II, which had no commonality with its namesake, was begun in 1926 as a contender for the next naval fighter require-ment. This design was not taken up, although the sole prototype did sea trials in *Furious* in July 1927. Eventually the chosen successor was the Hawker Nimrod/Osprey duo. It is pleasant to look at this as confirmation of the impossibility of finding a single type which could replace the Flycatcher . . . of such stuff are legends made.

Fairey Flycatcher: *Span* 29 ft 0 in; *Length* 23 ft 0 in; *Height* 12 ft 0 in; *Wing area* 288 sq ft; *Engine* One 400 hp Armstrong Siddeley Jaguar IV; *All up weight* 3,028 lb; *Maximum speed* 134 mph at sea level; *Service ceiling* 20,600 ft; *Range* 311 miles; *Armament* 2 × 0.303 in Vickers machine-guns on sides of fuselage 4 × 20 lb bombs under wings.

Fairey IIIF

With a first flight on March 19 1926 there appeared the most prolific variant of the Fairey III series. More than 600 examples were constructed before the last delivery in September 1932 and of these more than half were delivered to the Fleet Air Arm. Norman Macmillan was at the controls for the first flight of the IIIF prototype, which differed from the preceeding IIID most noticeably in its cleaner fuselage lines. The fin and rudder were also of different outline in the early marks of the IIIF series, though still with the squared-off look typical of Fairey aircraft of that period. In the later, more prolific marks, the fin took on a smooth curve to its leading edge with the top line continuing across the top of the rudder. The initial production version for the FAA was the IIIF Mk I with the Napier Lion VA engine. This was followed by the IIIF Mk II which had the Lion XI and a slightly increased all up weight. What might be considered the definitive naval variant was the Fairey IIIF Mk IIIM which had an all-metal structure (earlier marks had wooden wings) and the Napier Lion XIA engine. The final seagoing variant was the Mk IIIB which was strengthened for catapulting and was operated from the catapults of several capital ships, including the battlecruiser *Hood*.

Initial deck landing trials were made aboard *Furious* in 1927, using one of a pre-production batch converted on the line from the final IIID order. No arrester hook was fitted in the IIIF during its carrier-borne service but a trial installation under the rear fuselage was made in a Mk III for tests with transverse arrestor wires in *Courageous* during 1931. This system proved satisfactory and thenceforward became the standard for carrier operations. The first unit to receive IIIFs was No 440 Flight in 1927. The next year saw the two spotter-reconnaissance flights belonging to *Courageous*, Nos 445 and 446, forming on the type and a steady flow of aircraft spread through the carrier fleet by the beginning of the 30s. With April 1933 came the rearrangement of Fleet Air Arm flights into squadrons. Five units were operational on Fairey IIIFs—No 820 Squadron in *Courageous*, 822 in *Furious*, 823 and 825 in *Glorious* and 824 in *Eagle*.

Most of the carrier-borne IIIFs had wheel under-carriages. However, in 1930, experiments were

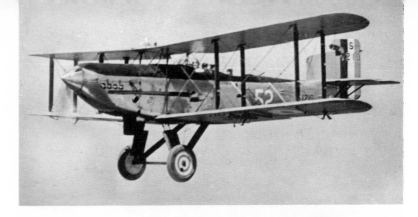

Right *Fairey IIIF Mk II flying from HMS* Furious (Bruce Robertson).

Right *Fairey IIIF Mk III—note the revised fin shape.*

Right *Fairey IIID of 440 Flight has its fleet number on a black panel, the carrier colour of HMS* Eagle (Bruce Robertson).

made on *Furious'* flight deck to test the practicability of landing and taking off on floats. Presumably, the theory behind this idea was to enable the launch and recovery of floatplanes without having to stop the ship to lift the aircraft on to and off the water. Anyway, the trials led to nothing and the practice proved somewhat risky as there was difficulty in keeping the aircraft straight, particularly on landing.

Not long after formation, No 820 Squadron began to replace its IIIFs with the succeeding aircraft from the same stable, the Fairey Seal, probably operating both types during the transition.

Fairey IIIF Mk IIIM/B: *Span* 45 ft 9 in (14 ft 3 in folded); *Length* 34 ft 0 in; *Height* 12 ft 9 in; *Wing area* 443 sq ft; *Engine* One 570 hp Napier Lion XIA; *All up weight* 5,874 lb; *Maximum speed* 136 mph at 10,000 ft; *Service ceiling* 20,000 ft; *Endurance* 3–4 hours; *Armament* 1 × 0.303 in Vickers machine gun fixed forward-firing and 1 × 0.303 in Lewis machine-gun on flexible mount in rear cockpit, up to 500 lb of bombs on wing racks (or extra fuel tanks).

Above S1564 *began life as the Blackburn Ripon II illustrated. As with the other 21 in the batch it was converted into a Baffin.*

Left *Ripon II* S1465 *dropping a torpedo* (Nigel B. Leicester).

Right *A flight of Baffins, all of which were originally produced as Ripons and converted. The leading aircraft went on to serve in the RNZAF* (Bruce Robertson).

Blackburn Ripon and Baffin

Taking their torpedo biplane design a step further, Blackburn reworked the Dart to specification 21/23, which demanded a much greater range for the purpose of adding a reconnaissance role to the aircraft's capability. Of roughly similar dimensions to the Dart, the new T.5 design was to be a two-seater because of the need for an observer/navigator to reduce the burden on the pilot on long range recce missions. The first prototype of the T.5, which was named Ripon, took to the air on April 17 1926 and a second aircraft with a float undercarriage followed shortly afterwards. Competitive trials against the Handley Page Harrow resulted in the advancement of the Blackburn machine with a third prototype being ordered. When this emerged, the overall design had changed completely from that of the earlier pair of prototypes, the Ripon II having generally much finer lines and the more powerful Lion XI engine.

A production batch was ordered and deliveries commenced in 1929 with 462 Flight being first to equip in July. Two further sub-variants followed the initial production; the Ripon IIA introduced Handley Page slots on the upper wing and the IIC had all-metal wings with an increased angle of sweepback. Production continued up to the end of 1933. The licensed production by Finland of the Ripon IIF, equipped with various radial engines, led to the introduction of the B-5 Baffin to the Fleet Air Arm. Under the designation T.5J Ripon V, two airframes were equipped with radial engines for trials, one with an Armstrong Siddeley Tiger and the other with a Bristol Pegasus. The Pegasus-powered version was selected for production to specification 4/33, 29 aircraft being built new as Baffins and about 65 Ripons being converted to the new radial powerplant subsequently. The Ripon-equipped 461 and 462 Flights embarked in *Glorious* were amalgamated to form 812 Squadron in 1933 and the new unit was the first to receive Baffins in January 1934. The Baffin's service career only lasted three years, with No 812 Squadron the last to relinquish the type at the end of 1936. The type's successors were the Blackburn Shark in 810 Squadron and the Fairey Swordfish in 811 and 812.

Blackburn Ripon II: *Span* 44 ft 10 in (17 ft 10 in folded); *Length* 36 ft 9 in; *Height* 13 ft 4 in; *Wing area* 683 sq ft; *Engine* One 570 hp Napier Lion XIA; *All up weight* 7,405 lb; *Maximum speed* 126 mph at sea level; *Service ceiling* 10,000 ft; *Range* 815 miles with torpedo, 1,060 miles for reconnaissance; *Armament* 1 × 0.303 in Vickers machine-gun fixed forward-firing and 1 × 0.303 in Lewis machine-gun on flexible mount in aft cockpit, 1 × Mk VIII or X torpedo or 3 × 250 lb bombs or 3 × 550 lb bombs.

Blackburn Baffin: *Span* 45 ft 6½ in (17 ft 10 in folded); *Length* 38 ft 3¾ in; *Height* 13 ft 5½ in; *Wing area* 683 sq ft; *Engine* One 565 hp Bristol Pegasus I.M3; *All up weight* 7,610 lb; *Maximum speed* 136 mph at 6,500 ft; *Service ceiling* 15,000 ft; *Range* 450 miles; *Armament* 1 × 0.303 in Vickers machine-gun fixed forward-firing and 1 × 0.303 in Lewis machine-gun on flexible mount in aft cockpit, 1 × 1,570 lb Mk VIII or X torpedo or 1 × 2,000 lb bomb or 6 × 250 lb bombs or 3 × 550 lb bombs.

Hawker Osprey

Developed from the Hawker Hart light bomber to specification 0.22/26, the Hawker Osprey was the first fighter-reconnaissance type to enter naval service. Although its role was so described, its chief function was reconnaissance, particularly when operated in its floatplane configuration from the catapults of cruisers. From aircraft carriers the Osprey usually operated in concert with its stable-mate the Nimrod fighter, a combination of these two types being flown by each flight or squadron. The first flying trials were made in 1930 from Brooklands with the original Hart prototype fitted with folding wings, followed by tests on a twin float undercarriage from the MAEE Felixstowe. Two Osprey prototypes were ordered in 1931 and production was soon underway. Four mark variations were distinguished chiefly by the installation of different versions of the Kestrel engine and additional items of equipment such as an engine-driven generator, upper wing dinghy stowage and change from wooden to metal propeller.

Ospreys (and Nimrods) began to replace Flycatchers in 404 Flight in *Courageous* and re-equipped No 409 Flight for service in *Glorious* towards the end of 1932. Several adventures came the way of the Ospreys of *Hermes'* No 803 Squadron operating on the China Station from 1935, when they were called upon to deal with the depredations of the local pirate populations. Three years later, this same unit saw a brief spell aboard the newly completed *Ark Royal* before being replaced by the Blackburn Skua.

Hawker Osprey IV: *Span* 37 ft 0 in (15 ft 7¼ in folded); *Length* 29 ft 4 in; *Height* 10 ft 5 in; *Wing area* 339 sq ft; *Engine* One 640 hp Rolls-Royce Kestrel V; *All up weight* 4,970 lb; *Maximum speed* 176 mph at 13,120 ft; *Service ceiling* 25,000 ft; *Endurance* 2¼ hours; *Armament* 1 × 0.303 in Vickers machine-gun fixed forward-firing and 1 × 0.303 in Lewis machine-gun on flexible mount in aft cockpit.

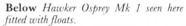

Left Hawker Osprey S1698 of 803 Squadron at Seletar in 1937.

Below Hawker Osprey Mk 1 seen here fitted with floats.

Hawker Nimrod

When specification N.21/26 was issued in 1926 the aircraft called for was to be a replacement for the Fairey Flycatcher. At that time Hawker had available their Hoopoe private venture prototype and this was evaluated as a contender for the requirement, which was destined not to be met by any of the competitors. However, the trials led to the development by Hawker of a new design similar in basic layout to the Fury but with essential refinements needed for a naval fighter, including flotation bags in the rear fuselage and flotation boxes built into the upper wing near the tips. The engine was to be the Rolls-Royce Kestrel 12-cylinder in-line. Work had been started on construction of this aeroplane when a further specification (16/30) was issued giving official recognition of the type's development as a fleet fighter. No name had yet been allocated for the new aircraft though it was known unofficially by Hawker as the Norn (from

Norse mythology—due to Danish interest) and bore the company registration H.N.1. First flight was made early in 1930, followed by preliminary trials which led to the placing of an initial production order for 12 Nimrods. The first of these was to be H.N.1 reworked to production standard. Before that happened, however, the prototype had been taken to Buenos Aires in the aircraft carrier *Eagle* to appear in the British Empire Trade Exhibition of March 1931.

The first Nimrod (rebuilt H.N.1) flew on October 14 1931, bearing the serial number *S1577* and proceeded with official trials at Martlesham Heath, while the second aircraft went to Felixstowe to explore the type's handling qualities when equipped with floats. In April 1932, deck trials were made in *Eagle* and the Nimrod was cleared for service in June. No 408 Flight, allocated to *Glorious*, was the first unit to receive Nimrods, replacing their Flycatchers. The next year's reorganisation of the Fleet Air Arm saw the formation of the 800-series of

Right K2911, *a stainless steel Nimrod Mk II of 801 Squadron, caught by an arrestor wire.*

Below *Fleet Air Arm training in the '30s was given by No 1 Flying Training School, RAF Leuchars. Here a fleet pilot is undergoing catapulted take-off in Nimrod K3654 which later served in 802 FAA Squadron (Bruce Robertson).*

first-line squadrons, No 408 Flight joining with No 409, both in *Glorious*, to form No 802 Squadron. Other Nimrod squadrons emerging were 800 in *Courageous* and 801 in *Furious*. The third production batch, beginning with *K2823*, introduced a V-frame arrester hook under the rear fuselage. *K2823* itself was retained by Hawker for modification as the Nimrod (Intermediate) with swept back wings, this being the prototype for the Nimrod II which entered production in September 1933. No 802 Squadron, first to receive Nimrods, became the last to lose them when they were replaced by Sea Gladiators in May 1939.

Hawker Nimrod I: *Span* 33 ft 6$\frac{1}{4}$ in; *Length* 26 ft 11$\frac{3}{4}$ in; *Height* 9 ft 9 in; *Wing area* 298.5 sq ft; *Engine* One 590 hp Rolls-Royce Kestrel IIS; *All up weight* 4,258 lb; *Maximum speed* 196 mph at 12,000 ft; *Service ceiling* 25,000 ft; *Endurance* 1 hour 40 minutes; *Armament* 2 × 0.303 in Vickers machine-guns fixed forward-firing 4 × 20 lb bombs on rack under starboard wing.

Fairey Seal

Bringing to an end the Fairey IIIF design sequence, the Fairey Seal was at first known as the Fairey IIIF Mk VI. The chief difference was the replacing of the in-line Napier Lion engine with a 14-cylinder two-row radial, the Armstrong Siddeley Panther IIA. Other different features of the Seal were an arrester hook fitted as standard from the outset, a tail wheel in place of the IIIF's skid and a new fin and rudder. A IIIF Mk IIIB was fitted with the Panther engine to serve as a prototype and completed its first flight on September 11 1930 in the hands of C. S. Staniland. This IIIF was then fully converted to the Mk VI standard and flown again as such on November 27 1931. Further test flying took place in 1932 with a twin-float undercarriage. Seals so equipped were to succeed IIIFs in the catapult flights embarked in capital ships. Deliveries of production aircraft to the Fleet Air Arm started in 1933 and after the usual service trials, began to re-equip the spotter-reconnaissance squadrons in the fleet's aircraft carriers. *Courageous'* No 820 and 821 Squadrons were the first units involved. The Seal was the Navy's last dedicated spotter-recce type in first line service as the role subsequently was to be merged with that of fighter or torpedo bomber. In 1935, the Blackburn Shark replaced the Seals of 820 Squadron and those of 821 were replaced the following year. 821's Seals were handed over to 822 Squadron in *Furious* replacing that unit's IIIFs. The three remaining carrier-borne squadrons, plus No 825 shore-based, re-formed on the Shark's rival, the Fairey Swordfish, between 1936 and 1938.

Fairey Seal: *Span* 45 ft 9 in (14 ft 3 in folded); *Length* 33 ft 8 in; *Height* 12 ft 9 in; *Wing area* 443.5 sq ft; *Engine* One 525 hp Armstrong Siddeley Panther IIA; *All up weight* 6,000 lb; *Maximum speed* 138 mph; *Service ceiling* 17,000 ft; *Endurance* 4$\frac{1}{2}$ hours; *Armament* 1 × 0.303 in Vickers machine-gun fixed forward-firing and 1 × 0.303 in Lewis machine-gun on flexible mount in rear cockpit, up to 500 lb of bombs under wings.

Fairey Seal K4779 exhibits the fin and rudder, an identity feature of the type.

Above *Blackburn Shark 1 K4357 prior to delivery to 820 Squadron.*

Right *Blackburn Shark prototype K4295, the warren girder style of interplane struts clearly to be seen.*

Blackburn Shark

The Shark brought to an end the Blackburn line of biplane torpedo bombers. A contemporary of the Fairey Swordfish, and largely overshadowed by that aeroplane, the Blackburn Shark stemmed from the private venture B-6 prototype which was designed to meet specification S.15/33 by Major F. A. Bumpus. This machine first flew on August 24 1933 at Brough and was evaluated at A & AEE Martlesham Heath before the end of the year. Trials aboard *Courageous* in 1934 led to an order being placed for a production batch of 16 Shark Mk Is, some of which were delivered to Gosport in May 1935 for working up with No 820 Squadron, embarked in *Courageous*. A feature which met with the approval of the squadron armourers was that the bomb racks could be loaded with the wings folded before despatching the aircraft up the lift to the flight deck.

The prototype was reworked to improve standard, including a 760 hp Tiger VI engine in place of the 700 hp Tiger IV, to introduce the Shark Mk II which entered production in 1935 and began to equip two more squadrons the following year,

Nos 810 and 821. The first-line career of the Shark ended in 1938 when all three squadrons took Swordfish on charge and the Blackburn biplane was relegated to shore-based training duties. This was a role that was to last well into the Second World War, the British Air Observers School at Piarco, Trinidad, operating Shark Mk IIIs as late as 1944. The Mark III, which had a glazed canopy over the cockpit, did not see carrier-borne duty but the 1937 production batch gave useful service in the training and target-towing roles. The type was also built by Canada's Boeing Aircraft factory in Vancouver for service with the Royal Canadian Air Force.

Blackburn Shark Mk II: *Span* 46 ft 0 in (15 ft 0 in folded); *Length* 35 ft 2¼ in; *Height* 12 ft 1 in; *Wing area* 489 sq ft; *Engine* One 760 hp Armstrong Siddeley Tiger VI; *All up weight* 8,050 lb; *Maximum speed* 152 mph at 6,500 ft; *Service ceiling* 16,400 ft; *Range* 625 miles; *Armament* 1 × 0.303 in Vickers machine-gun fixed forward-firing and 1 × 0.303 in Lewis machine-gun or Vickers gas-operated gun on flexible mount in rear cockpit, 1 × 1,500 lb torpedo or up to 2,000 lb of bombs under the wings.

Fairey Swordfish

The Swordfish's origins date back to the early 30s when a private venture aircraft designed by Marcel Lobelle, Fairey's chief designer, was built as a potential torpedo bomber or spotter reconnaissance machine. Known by the company as 'the Greek machine' because of the hope that that country would order the aircraft for its navy, it first flew on March 21 1933 from Harmondsworth airfield in the hands of test pilot C. S. Staniland. Unfortunately, the aircraft was lost six months later when it had to be abandoned in flight after Staniland had found himself unable to get out of a flat spin. Shortly before this mishap, British specification S.15/33 had been issued, for which it was thought the private venture machine would be suitable. Undaunted by the loss, the Fairey design team produced a second aircraft to comply with the terms of the specification, and this, known as the TSR II (torpedo-spotter-reconnaissance number two) and serialled *K4190*, was in the air for the first time on April 17 1934. Trials at the A & AEE Martlesham Heath brought to light a number of features needing attention, including stall and spinning characteristics. With these problems rectified, the new specification S.38/34 was draughted to cover the revised TSR II. Just over a year after the first flight,

an order was placed for 86 production aircraft plus a batch of three development aircraft.

Production proceeded apace, owing to the uncomplicated nature of the design, with deliveries to the Fleet Air Arm beginning in the early summer of 1936. The first squadron to equip was No 825, which replaced its Fairey Seals with Swordfish in July. Squadrons 811 and 812 followed suit, these units changing over from Blackburn Baffins, another type to be succeeded by the Swordfish. By the end of 1938, the Swordfish had become the Navy's sole torpedo bomber with the Blackburn Shark being the last of its predecessors to go, from Nos 810, 820 and 821 Squadrons. A total of 13 front line units was equipped by September 1939, with 12 of that number embarked in the fleet's carriers.

The wartime career of the Swordfish was so extensive that only a few examples of its achievements can be recorded in this entry. Books can be, and have been, written on this epic-making aircraft which served on ship and shore and with the Royal Air Force as well as the Navy. The first successful action by the 'Stringbag' was not actually achieved by one of the carrier-borne squadrons but by one of the float-equipped machines belonging to the battleship *Warspite*. On April 13 1940, when *Warspite* and her accompanying destroyers made the second attack on Narvik, the Swordfish was

Fairey Swordfish L9781 *circles the wartime HMS* Ark Royal.

Rocket projectiles could be fitted on the underwing racks of the Swordfish II (British Aerospace).

catapulted to spot the dispositions of the enemy vessels. This was carried out with such success that seven German destroyers were eliminated. Not only that, but the Swordfish sank the submarine *U.64* by dive-bombing on the same operation, thus chalking up the FAA's first U-boat of the war.

As for Taranto, this was to prove to the Japanese that what they wanted to do at Pearl Harbor was a practical possibility. On November 11 1940, Swordfish of *Illustrious*' 815 and 819 Squadrons, together with five aircraft detached from *Eagle*'s 813 and 824, took off to attempt to neutralise the potential Italian naval threat to Allied operations in the Mediterranean. Despite the very heavy anti-aircraft defences surrounding the anchorage, the Swordfish successfully penetrated the screen of balloons, searchlights and gunfire to sink one

battleship and to cripple two more, as well as damaging two cruisers and two destroyers and sinking two auxiliaries. Only two Stringbags were lost.

In May 1941, when the German battleship *Bismarck* set out on her famous sortie, it was to be the Swordfish that would bring her to heel. In severe weather, the first torpedo attack was mounted by 825 Squadron flying from *Victorious*. Only one hit was obtained forward, which caused the ship to trim by the bow, though this did not greatly impede her progress. *Victorious* was compelled to withdraw from the action as fuel was running low. Meanwhile *Ark Royal* was proceeding as quickly as weather would allow, north from Gibraltar, with 810, 818 and 820 Squadrons.

On May 26, the carrier was within range and the

Perhaps the best known of all Swordfish torpedo bombers is NF389 *regularly flying with the Fleet Air Arm. Here it is shown with its wings folded* (Mike Bowyer).

first attack was launched in the early afternoon. The magnetic setting of the torpedoes' pistols caused the 'fish' to explode as they entered the water. Luckily this assisted the escape of their target—the cruiser *Sheffield* had been attacked in error. A second attempt was made that afternoon with the torpedoes' pistols set to explode on contact. This time they found *Bismarck* and scored two hits, one of which was vital. The torpedo struck right aft damaging the steering gear and jamming the rudders. Now largely unmanoeuvrable, *Bismarck* was at the mercy of the fast closing big-gun ships.

On February 12 1942, Swordfish of No 825 Squadron, shore-based at RAF Manston, carried out a suicidal mission in an attempt to delete from Hitler's inventory the *Scharnhorst, Gneisenau* and *Prinz Eugen*, which were making their infamous Channel Dash from Brest back to Germany. All six aircraft were lost for no visible effect on the ships but for the sheer cold courage shown in the attack, a posthumous award of the Victoria Cross was made to the CO of the Squadron, Lieutenant Commander Eugene Esmonde.

After 692 Swordfish had been constructed by Fairey, production responsibility was passed to Blackburn in 1940 and was to continue unabated until August 1944 when an overall total of 2,391 had been built. With the appearance of the escort carriers for convoy protection, the Swordfish began to operate from their decks in the anti-submarine role, starting with one flight of 825 Squadron aboard *Avenger* in September 1941. The weaponry carried by the Swordfish changed from the torpedo to the bomb and the rocket. To carry the latter, the underside of the lower mainplane was skinned in metal to allow the structure to withstand the burst of

flame when the rockets were fired. This new model was the Swordfish Mk II and the adoption of air-to-surface-vessel (ASV) radar brought the Mark III into being.

The basic airframe of the Swordfish remained unchanged throughout. Operating from the small decks of escort carriers and the later merchant aircraft carriers (MAC-Ships) was fraught with danger, the more so as convoys could not wait for fine weather to carry their vital cargoes. In an attempt to get the Swordfish airborne with greater rapidity, a further modification allowed the fitting of rocket assisted take-off gear (RATOG) beneath the fuselage. This was to prove valuable in take-offs from steeply pitching escort carriers' flight decks. The problem of getting down again remained however, and many a Swordfish suffered damage or was lost due to that insurmountable problem. Fittingly, the last Fleet Air Arm squadron to relinquish its Swordfish was the MAC-Ship Pool squadron, No 836, which disbanded on May 21 1945.

Fairey Swordfish I: *Span* 45 ft 6 in (17 ft 3 in folded); *Length* 36 ft 1 in; *Height* 12 ft 10½ in; *Wing area* 607 sq ft; *Engine* One 690 hp Bristol Pegasus III.M3; *All up weight* 8,700 lb; *Maximum speed* 139 mph at 4,750 ft; *Service ceiling* 12,400 ft; *Range* 546 miles; *Armament* 1 × 0.303 in Vickers machine-gun fixed forward-firing and 1 × 0.303 in Lewis machine-gun on flexible mount in rear cockpit, 1 × 18 in torpedo or up to 1,500 lb of bombs in various combinations of 500- and 250-pounders or 1 × 1,500 lb sea mine (Later marks equipped to carry 8 × 60 lb rocket projectiles or 25 lb solid-head armour-piercing projectiles and ASV radar mounted between undercarriage legs).

Blackburn Skua

The Skua's main claim to fame was achieved as a land-based aircraft rather than a carrier-borne one. On April 10 1940, 16 Skuas, seven from No 800 Squadron and nine from 803, flew from Hatston in the Orkneys to carry out a dive-bombing attack on the German cruiser *Königsberg* moored in Bergen harbour. Flying to the extreme of their range, the Skuas set off during the night to arrive at dawn over the target 330 miles away. Despite defensive fire, the attack was made with such fortune that the *Königsberg* was sunk for the loss of only one of her assailants. The two squadrons involved normally formed part of the complement of *Ark Royal*, having been temporarily disembarked in January 1940. Sadly, less than a fortnight after their triumph, having rejoined the *Ark Royal*, both squadrons were decimated in the ill-fated Narvik fighting.

The Blackburn Skua was conceived by G. E. Petty to meet the 1934 specification 0.27/34 which called for a fighter-reconnaissance-dive-bomber. With power from a single Bristol Mercury engine, the aircraft was to have an armament of four 0.303 in Browning Mk II machine guns mounted in the wings and a single 0.303 in Lewis gun on a pillar mount in the aft cockpit, to serve it in the fighter role. For dive-bombing a 500 lb semi-armour-piercing (SAP) bomb was to be carried on under-fuselage ejector arms, the bomb itself being semi-recessed into the aircraft's belly. In the diving attack, the arms would swing down to let the bomb fall clear of the propeller arc. There was also a pair of under wing carriers, each of which could take four 30 lb practice bombs.

The first of two prototypes flew for the first time from Brough in the hands of Flight Lieutenant A. M. Blake on February 9 1937, by which time a production batch of 190 had been ordered off the drawing board. Unfortunately, the Bristol Mercury engine was destined to power the prototypes only, because all production of that engine was required for the Bristol Blenheim bomber. It was to be replaced by the Bristol Perseus, which was to leave the Skua somewhat low on power. Notwithstanding this drawback, aircraft were delivered to Worthy Down towards the end of 1938 to re-equip 800 Squadron for *Ark Royal*. The following year *Furious'* 801 Squadron and 803, belonging to *Ark Royal*, also re-equipped with the Skua.

Shortly after the outbreak of the Second World War, on September 25 1939, a Skua of 803 Squadron succeeded in shooting down a Dornier Do 18 flying boat which was one of three shadowing *Ark Royal*. This was the first enemy aircraft to be brought down in an air-to-air encounter during the war. Not long afterwards, *Ark Royal* left home waters to serve on South Atlantic convoy protection duties based at Freetown, Sierra Leone.

The second prototype Blackburn Skua, K5179.

Gloster Sea Gladiator N5525 (MoD).

Addition of a four-gun Boulton Paul power-operated turret to the basic Skua design produced the Blackburn Roc, which was unsuccessful in its intended role of fleet fighter owing to the greater all up weight reducing performance to unacceptable levels. As a result the Roc was relegated to second-line duties.

When No 800 Squadron replaced its Skuas with Fairey Fulmar fighters in March 1941, the end of its carrier-borne service had been reached. From then onwards its role was reduced to training and target towing.

Blackburn Skua: *Span* 46 ft 2 in (16 ft 2 in folded); *Length* 35 ft 7 in; *Height* 14 ft 2 in; *Wing area* 312 sq ft; *Engine* One 830 hp Bristol Perseus XII; *All up weight* 8,230 lb; *Maximum speed* 225 mph at 6,700 ft; *Service ceiling* 19,100 ft; *Range* 760 miles; *Armament* 4 × 0.303 in Browning Mk II machine-guns in the wings and 1 × 0.303 in Lewis Mk IIIE machine-gun in aft cockpit, 1 × 500 lb SAP bomb.

Gloster Sea Gladiator

With the onset of a European war almost a certainty, the Royal Navy was most anxious to equip the Fleet Air Arm with a new fighter type as a replacement for the Hawker Nimrod, and to tide them over until the Blackburn Skua was ready. The first step was to modify 38 Gloster Gladiator II aircraft from the production line at Hucclecote as Sea Gladiators (Interim) by fitting arrester hooks and naval radio. These were delivered to shore bases for initial training in December 1938 while fully navalised machines were produced for carrier flying. The main alterations to the Gladiator to fit it for use at sea, apart from the hook and radio, were the addition of a dinghy in a fairing between the under-carriage legs, provision of cartridge case ejection chutes and modification of the ammunition belt box lids for the fuselage guns to allow refilling from within the aircraft. It was also planned that the armament would be increased by the addition of two more Browning guns in the upper wing but these had not passed service release trials before the squadrons went to sea and were not used operationally.

In March 1939, four Sea Gladiators carried out deck trials in *Courageous*. Soon afterwards that ship embarked 801 Squadron and 802 went aboard *Glorious*. No 801 was re-equipped with Skuas and assigned to *Furious* on the outbreak of war in September but *Glorious* operated in the Mediterranean briefly, before being sent to the Indian Ocean in October to protect the trade routes. She was recalled the following spring and assigned to cover naval operations off Norway, being sunk on June 8 when caught by the *Scharnhorst* and *Gneisenau*. A third squadron, No 804, had been equipped with Sea Gladiators for shore-based defence of Scapa Flow. A brief period was spent with *Glorious* off Norway but the unit had been transferred before her loss to *Furious*, to cover Atlantic ferrying operations. The only other squadron to operate Sea Gladiators from a carrier's deck was No 813. This was a Swordfish unit in *Eagle*, operating in the Mediterranean, and a fighter flight was formed from three or four Sea Gladiators which had been left in Alexandria as reserve aircraft for *Glorious'* 802 Squadron. They were put to good use, claiming the destruction of seven enemy aircraft during their period with the ship. Two were briefly transferred to *Illustrious* for the Taranto operation in November 1940. They were put ashore in Egypt in March 1941, thus ending the sea going career of the type.

Gloster Sea Gladiator: *Span* 32 ft 3 in; *Length* 27 ft 5 in; *Height* 11 ft 7 in; *Wing area* 323 sq ft; *Engine* One 830 hp Bristol Mercury VIIIA; *All up weight* 5,020 lb; *Maximum speed* 253 mph at 14,600 ft; *Service ceiling* 32,300 ft; *Range* 425 miles; *Armament* 4 × 0.303 in BSA/Browning machine-guns, two beneath lower wings and two in sides of fuselage.

Fairey Fulmar

On January 13 1937, C. S. Staniland, Fairey chief test pilot, flew the first prototype of a new light bomber, designed to meet specification P.4/34 as a replacement for the biplane Hawker Hart. By that date, however, the requirement had been cancelled. A second P.4/34 flew on April 19 1937 and in March 1938 was altered to serve as a flying mock-up of a new two-seat shipboard fighter, thus avoiding the need to build an all-new prototype and consequently saving considerable development time. This new design, to specification 0.8/38, was destined to give the Royal Navy its first successful monoplane carrier fighter, just in time to cover the vital Malta convoys of 1940. The first production Fulmar, as the type was named, flew at Ringway Airport, Manchester, on January 4 1940, and, together with the second aircraft, carried out initial trials at the A & AEE Boscombe Down. From the start, the production machines had the usual features necessary for a carrier fighter—folding wings, catapult spools and arrestor hook. They were

An early Fairey Fulmar Mk 1, N4015, photographed on Malta in 1943.

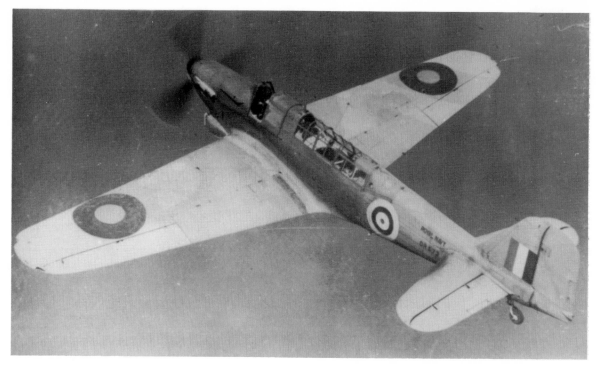

Fairey Fulmar II, DR673 *from the final production order.*

powered by the Rolls-Royce Merlin engine and had a wing-mounted armament of eight machine guns.

In May 1940, a Fulmar was delivered to the Service Trials Unit at Lee-on-Solent and the following month aircraft were equipping the first squadron, No 806, at Worthy Down. Wartime urgency had been splendidly met by the introduction of this new fighter and no time was lost in working up at sea with the carrier *Illustrious.* By September, the squadron was in action over the Mediterranean. A fine record of victories was recorded against the Italian bombers belabouring the convoys, No 808 Squadron in *Ark Royal* having joined the fray in October. From December 1940, the third Fulmar squadron, No 807, was to operate in the catapult fighter role from *Pegasus* (formerly the seaplane carrier *Ark Royal*) as one of the first elements of air cover for Atlantic convoys and No 804 followed suit in 1941, flying from *Springbank* and the catapult-equipped ocean boarding vessel, *Ariguani.*

Carrier-borne Fulmars were to provide fighter cover for many of the operations of the years 1941 and 1942, ranging from the North Cape (Norway) to the assault on Ceylon. In Crete, land-based Fulmars of No 805 Squadron were involved in the unsuccessful attempt to defend the island against the German invasion in the spring of 1941 and in Egypt, No 889 Squadron flew sorties over the Suez Canal Zone.

Although not equipped with dual controls, the good handling qualities of the aircraft suited it for use as a deck-landing trainer at a time when no other type was available, and from mid-1942 Fulmars were flying in this role from *Argus.* Use of the type in arid climes, with their dusty environments, led to the development of the tropicalised Fulmar II with an uprated Merlin engine and dust filters. In 1943, the Fulmar began to be replaced by other types, notably the Seafire, but some of the Fairey fighters soldiered on into the following year with 813 Squadron in the escort carrier *Campania.* She operated a combined complement of Swordfish, Wildcat and Fulmar in the protection of Gibraltar convoys.

Fairey Fulmar I: *Span* 46 ft 4½ in (17 ft 10 in folded); *Length* 40 ft 3 in; *Height* 14 ft 0 in; *Wing area* 342 sq ft; *Engine* One 1,080 hp Rolls-Royce Merlin VIII; *All up weight* 9,800 lb; *Maximum speed* 256 mph at 2,400 ft; *Service ceiling* 22,400 ft; *Range* 830 miles; *Armament* 8 × 0.303 in Browning machine-guns plus 2 × 250 lb bombs or 2 × 100 lb anti-submarine bombs.

Fairey Albacore

In 1936, specification S.41/36 was written, calling for a torpedo-bomber-reconnaissance aircraft to replace the Fairey Swordfish. Fairey's response for a Stringbag successor was a more refined biplane, to be powered by the Bristol Taurus 14-cylinder sleeve valve engine, with a fully enclosed, heated cockpit and performance-enhancing features such as a variable pitch propeller, automatic leading edge slats and hydraulically operated flaps which would double as dive brakes. An initial batch of one hundred Albacores, as the type was named, was ordered off the drawing board in May 1937, the first two of them to serve as prototypes. It was hoped to get the aircraft into service in the early part of 1939 but development problems with the engine were to frustrate this. The first prototype made its maiden flight on December 12 1938.

Deliveries to squadrons at last began in March 1940. On March 15, 12 aircraft were taken on charge by No 826 Squadron at Ford, this unit having been newly formed specifically to introduce the Albacore to service. First action was to be seen as a shore-based unit, when, on the last day of May

1940, the Albacores attacked German coastal shipping and road and rail transport in Belgium in a vain attempt to stem the westward tide of the Blitzkrieg. This was followed by some six months' operations with Coastal Command before 826 embarked in the aircraft carrier *Formidable*, together with 829 Squadron which had formed on Albacores in June at Lee-on-Solent. In February 1941, *Formidable* sailed for the Indian Ocean but was diverted to the Mediterranean to do battle with the Axis forces in the seas around Crete. On March 28 1941, Albacores flew torpedo strikes against units of the Italian fleet off Cape Matapan, obtaining a hit on the flagship *Vittorio Veneto* against heavy defensive fire. Dive-bombing attacks on Cretan airfields were another task the Albacores carried out. On May 26, *Formidable* received damage in an attack by the Luftwaffe, necessitating her withdrawal from the area for repairs. No 826 Squadron was put ashore and operated from desert airstrips in North Africa, whence it made night bombing attacks on the Afrika Korps.

In July 1941, Albacore squadrons flying from the carriers *Furious* and *Victorious* took part in attacks on the port installations at Petsamo and Kirkenes on the border between Norway and Finland, receiving a severe mauling in the process. Another debacle occurred in the attack made by *Victorious*' aircraft against the battleship *Tirpitz* in March 1942. The

The fifth Fairey Albacore bears Type B roundels, applied to Albacores early 1940 (Imperial War Museum).

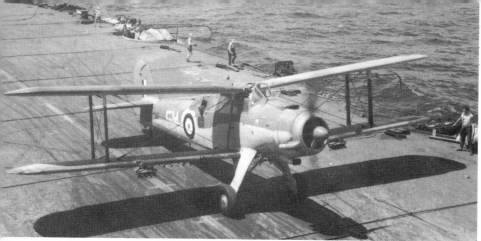

slow-flying Albacores presented a steady target when making their torpedo dropping runs. However, Albacores still had a useful part to play in support of the Allied landings, beginning in November 1942 with Operation *Torch* and subsequently at Sicily and Salerno. The latter operation saw the last use of the type as a carrier-borne aircraft, No 820 Squadron in *Formidable* being the unit involved. Shore-based units of the Fleet Air Arm, Royal Air Force and Royal Canadian Air Force carried on with the Albacore, the last named service's No 415 Squadron gaining a major victory with the sinking of the German torpedo boat *Greif* in the Baie de la Seine on May 24 1944.

Meanwhile, the carrier-borne squadrons had re-equipped with the monoplane Fairey Barracuda and Grumman Avenger.

Fairey Albacore: *Span* 50 ft 0 in; *Length* 39 ft 10 in; *Height* 14 ft 2 in: *Wing area* 623 sq ft; *Engine* One 1,085 hp Bristol Taurus XII; *All up weight* 11,186 lb; *Maximum speed* 161 mph at 4,500 ft; *Service ceiling* 20,700 ft; *Range* 930 miles; *Armament* 1 × 0.303 in Browning machine-gun in starboard lower mainplane and 1 × 0.303 in Vickers 'K' machine-gun in rear cockpit, plus 1 × 18 in torpedo or 3 × 500 lb bombs or 6 × 100 lb anti-submarine bombs plus 4 × 20 lb bombs or 6 × 250 lb bombs plus 4 × 20 lb bombs.

Hawker Sea Hurricane

During the Norwegian campaign, in May 1940, No 46 Squadron RAF had been taken aboard the carrier *Glorious* in the Clyde and ferried to a position off the coast of Norway. There the aircraft flew off to operate from land bases as air cover for ground forces fighting in the Narvik area. The weight of the German attack proved too much to hold off and the Allied forces were compelled to evacuate. No 46 Squadron flew on to *Glorious* to return home but the carrier had the misfortune to be caught and overwhelmed by the *Scharnhorst* and *Gneisenau*, all the aircraft being lost with the ship.

From this disaster emerged the fact that the Hawker Hurricane had proved able to operate from the deck of an aircraft carrier. Development ensued of a variant of the aircraft equipped to operate in a maritime role. This did not entail a great deal of work as the first version, the Sea Hurricane Mk IA, merely added catapult spools to second-hand Hurricane Is to enable them to be launched from rocket-powered catapults mounted over the foredeck of suitable cargo vessels. These CAM-Ships (Catapult Armed Merchant Ships) were produced to give a degree of defence to convoys against the Focke Wulf Fw 200 Condor maritime patrol aircraft and the 'Hurricats' and their pilots were supplied by the Merchant Ship Fighter Unit of

the RAF. For the Fleet Air Arm, No 804 Squadron operated Sea Hurricanes from the Fighter Catapult Ships of the Royal Navy. One from the *Maplin* was the first to shoot down an Fw 200C on August 3 1941.

Meanwhile, Sea Hurricane Mk IBs were being converted for flight deck operation. They were fitted with catapult spools and arrestor hooks, had fuselages strengthened and naval radio equipment fitted. No 880 Squadron was the first to equip, that unit's A Flight being embarked in *Furious* for the Petsamo and Kirkenes raids in July 1941. Nos 803 and 806 Squadrons' Sea Hurricanes operated from land bases in the Eastern Mediterranean from July 1941 till January 1942 as the Naval Fighter Squadron, flying in support of the Army in the defence of Egypt. The escort carrier *Avenger* embarked 802 and

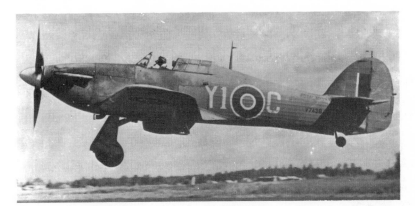

Right *Sea Hurricanes served in a variety of roles, the Mk 1 here,* V7438, *being used as a fighter trainer.*

Below *Hawker Sea Hurricane 1c (Merlin III) in April 1943.*

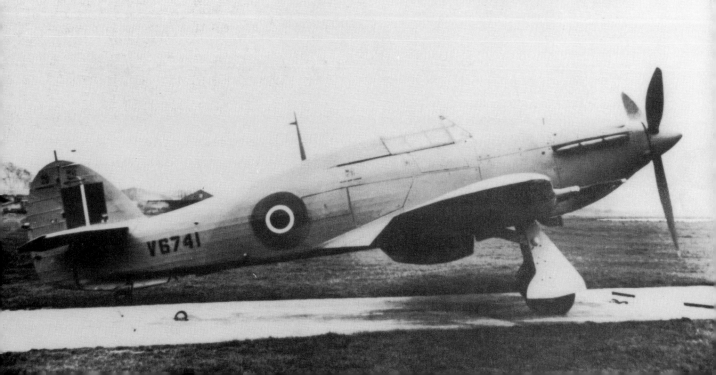

883 Squadrons in mid-1941 and operated with the Home Fleet until the end of 1942. During this period, the ship served as part of the carrier force covering the Operation *Torch* landings in French North-West Africa in November 1942. Carrier-borne Sea Hurricanes had first appeared in the Mediterranean when four had been allotted to *Eagle*'s Swordfish-equipped No 813 Squadron in March 1942. June saw *Eagle* taking part in the Operation *Harpoon* convoy to Malta. Her fighter complement, expanded by the Sea Hurricanes of No 801 Squadron, formed the chief element of the convoy's air cover.

At about the time of the Harpoon convoy, the Mark IC variant was equipping squadrons. This introduced a four 20 mm Hispano cannon armament in place of the eight Browning machine-guns of the earlier marks. Later in 1942 came the Sea Hurricane Mk IIC with a performance increase provided by the Merlin XX engine.

The Malta convoys reached their climax in August 1942 with Operation *Pedestal*. The powerful escort for this convoy, which contained the tanker *Ohio* and was to prove the key one for Malta's survival, included three fleet carriers—*Eagle, Indomitable* and *Victorious*. Amongst their complement were five squadrons equipped with Sea Hurricanes and these were to obtain the lion's share of victories in the aerial combats, despite the loss of 16 of their number when *Eagle* succumbed to four torpedoes from the submarine *U.73*. From this point onwards, the Sea Hurricane squadrons began to dwindle as conversion to the Seafire started, the original No 880 being re-equipped in time for the *Torch* landings in November. Nevertheless, the process was to be a slow one, as the final unit to relinquish its aircraft, No 824 Squadron, did not do so until April 1944. This unit was serving in the escort carrier *Striker* with 12 Swordfish and six Sea Hurricanes. The latter provided cover for the Swordfish in their raids on shipping along the Norwegian coast—fittingly in view of the type's origins and the area of their first action, nearly three years before.

Hawker Sea Hurricane Mk IIC: *Span* 40 ft 0 in; *Length* 32 ft $3\frac{3}{5}$ in; *Height* 13 ft $3\frac{3}{5}$ in; *Wing area* 257.5 sq ft; *Engine* One 1,460 hp Rolls-Royce Merlin XX; *All up weight* 7,800 lb; *Maximum speed* 342 mph at 22,000 ft; *Service ceiling* 35,600 ft; *Range* 460 miles (908 with two 44 gallon drop tanks); *Armament* 4 × 20 mm British Hispano Mk I or II cannon.

Grumman Wildcat

In 1939, the French government had placed an order with Grumman for a batch of 81 G-36As for the Marine Nationale. They would have served in the aircraft carrier *Béarn* and two other ships then building. However, none of the aircraft had been delivered to France by the time of the German invasion and they were quickly taken up by Britain to become the Fleet Air Arm's Grumman Martlet Is. Minor alterations were necessary, including the changing of the throttle linkages, which in French aircraft operated in reverse to British and American practice. The fuselage guns were to have been added when the aircraft arrived in France so in British service the Mk Is had only four wing-mounted Colt-Browning machine guns. Also the wings were non-folding. The aircraft were dismantled for shipping across the Atlantic, re-erection being carried out by Scottish Aviation at Prestwick. The first six Martlets arrived in August 1940 and one of these was sent to the A & AEE Boscombe Down for trials. In September, No 804 Squadron, shore-based at Hatston, became the first unit to receive Martlets, scoring the type's first combat victory when two aircraft caught an intruding Junkers Ju 88 on December 25 1940.

Two months earlier, the first of the British order for 100 G-36Bs had taken to the air. These were designated Martlet II and all except the first ten featured wing folding. The folding aircraft were equivalent to the US Navy's F4F-3 variant and shared the same wing armament of six 0.50 in guns. No 802 Squadron was equipped with Mark IIs and took them aboard the first British escort carrier, *Audacity*, in September 1941 to act as escort to Gibraltar convoys. On September 20, one of 802's Martlets brought down a Focke Wulf Fw 200, the first of several victories to be claimed before *Audacity* was torpedoed and sunk on December 21 by the submarine *U.751*.

Under a lend-lease agreement between Greece and the United States, a batch of 30 Grumman F4F-3As was to be delivered to the former country to help fight off the Italians, but, as in the French case, the aircraft had not been delivered before the German occupation occurred. Consequently these aircraft too were taken over by the Fleet Air Arm, operating from Egypt with No 805 Squadron as Martlet IIIs.

The Anglo-American lend-lease agreement of 1941 opened the doors to the American military manufacturing machine and amongst the flood of equipment made available were more of the Grumman fighters. The next version, the Martlet

Opposite page *Grumman Martlet IIs aboard a carrier. These aircraft were delivered with non-folding wings, but some were later modified for wing folding.* **Inset** *Grumman Martlets entered Fleet Air Arm service in 1940, an early example being depicted here.*

Left *An unusual feature of the Martlet was the mid-set wing.*

Above *Wildcat V* JV432 *wearing SEAC-style roundels taking off from HMS* Atheling. *Although largely ousted by more modern types, Wildcats played an important part in naval operations late in the war.*

IV, was equivalent to the F4F-4 except for the engine, which featured a single-stage, instead of a two-stage, supercharger. In 1943, production of the Wildcat (the original US Navy name allocated in October 1941 and adopted by Britain from January 1944) became the responsibility of the Eastern Aircraft Division of General Motors and the US designations for aircraft built by that company were FM-1 and FM-2. The latter was powered by the 9-cylinder single-row Cyclone engine as opposed to the previous version's 14-cylinder two-row Twin Wasp; both versions had only four wing guns. The FM-1 became the Wildcat V and the FM-2 the Wildcat VI in Fleet Air Arm service. That service was prolific and widespread. Apart from the Solomons, where *Victorious'* three Martlet-equipped squadrons operated in May–July 1943, the Pacific theatre was the only major area not to see the type in action in large numbers. The Arctic and Atlantic convoys, the Mediterranean and Aegean operations and patrols in the Indian Ocean all involved Martlets and Wildcats at some stage. More than two dozen squadrons operated the type from carrier decks, particularly from escort carriers where they often formed part of a mix of aircraft with torpedo bombers such as the Swordfish and Avenger.

Grumman Martlet/Wildcat IV: *Span* 38 ft 0 in (14 ft 4 in folded); *Length* 28 ft 11 in; *Height* 9 ft 2½ in; *Wing area* 260 sq ft; *Engine* One 1,200 hp Pratt & Whitney R-1830 Twin Wasp; *All up weight* 6,100 lb; *Maximum speed* 330 mph at 19,500 ft; *Service ceiling* 28,000 ft; *Range* 1,150 miles; *Armament* 6 × 0.50 in Browning machine-guns in the wings.

Supermarine Seafire

Just before Christmas 1941, a Supermarine Spitfire VB, serial number *AB205*, flown by Lieutenant Commander H. P. Bramwell, landed on board the carrier *Illustrious* in the Clyde. This aircraft, fitted with an A-frame arrester hook, was proving the feasibility of operating the distinguished fighter from the Royal Navy's aircraft carriers as a counter to the threat posed by the latest German high performance fighters such as the Focke Wulf Fw 190. Two hundred and fifty Spitfires were to be transferred to the Royal Navy and would be simply modified to suit them for seagoing use. This entailed the fitting of an arrester hook and fuselage slinging points, naval radio equipment and homing beacon receiver. The first modified aircraft were to be called Seafire Mk IB and they were to be quickly followed by the Seafire Mk IIC, which would have catapult spools fitted, whilst the Spitfire's 'C' wing gave provision for an extra pair of 20 mm cannon. In the event, this facility was not taken up, owing to loss of performance due to the weight of the two guns and their ammunition.

The first Seafires were delivered on June 15 1942 and No 807 was the first squadron to form later that month at Lee-on-Solent. Further squadrons quickly followed suit and were ready to take part in the North African landings in November. Five squadrons were present in the carriers *Argus*, *Furious*, *Victorious* and *Formidable*. The Seafires were chiefly involved in keeping at bay the Vichy French fighters, 807 claiming their first victim, a Dewoitine

Above *A formation of Seafire 1bs, Spitfire Vbs converted into Seafires.*

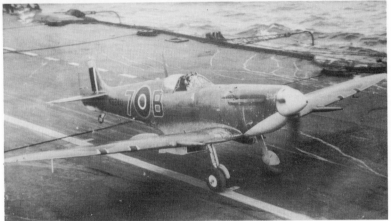

Right *Taking off, Seafire IIc MB240 carries only two of the possible four cannon. Machine-gun ports are taped over.*

Below *The Seafire XV was a naval adaptation of the first production Griffon Spitfire, the Mk XII. The second prototype, shown, was NS490.*

D.520, on November 8. They also strafed ground forces and airfields.

To improve performance, the Merlin 32 engine was substituted for the 45 or 46 model previously installed, raising output from 1,210 to 1,640 hp. Seafires thus equipped were designated L IIC. Earlier Seafires were converted to the new engine starting in March 1943 and No 807 was the first squadron to re-equip. Primary responsibility for development and production of the Seafire was given to Westland Aircraft with Cunliffe-Owen as chief sub-contractor. The next variant was the Seafire Mk III which introduced wing folding. Previously only *Argus* and *Furious* had been able to take Seafires into the protection of their hangars as they had large 'T' shaped lifts; the modern fleet carriers had to keep their Seafires, when embarked, in a deck park. This was not a satisfactory arrangement so folding wings were a great advantage. The main production version was the Seafire L.III, fitted with the low-altitude Merlin 55M engine which had individual ejector exhaust stacks giving a slight weight saving and an element of 'jet' thrust.

July 1943 brought the next major operation involving Seafires when 807, 880 and 899 Squadrons in *Indomitable*, together with 885 in *Formidable*, formed a part of the fighter cover for Operation *Husky*, the invasion of Sicily. Many deck-landing trials had been carried out, starting in September 1942 in *Biter*, to prepare the Seafire for operation from escort carriers. In September 1943,

SX137 *represents the third stage in naval Seafire development, the addition of a 'teardrop' canopy. This was a feature of the Griffon-powered Seafire XVII (Mike Bowyer).*

escort carrier-borne Seafires were in action for the first time in support of another landing, this time at Salerno in Southern Italy (Operation *Avalanche*). Six squadrons and two fighter flights were carried in the escort carriers *Attacker, Battler, Hunter* and *Stalker* and a further three Seafire squadrons were embarked in *Unicorn*, built as an aircraft maintenance ship but pressed into service as a carrier by virtue of the fact that she had a valuable flight deck.

Well over a third of the Seafires were written off in landing accidents and as a result further trials were undertaken to try to improve the landing characteristics of the type. Despite the drawbacks in deck landing performance, partly due to the narrow track undercarriage, service use in no way diminished. Seafires from *Furious* were involved in tactical strikes in Norwegian waters from the winter of 1943/44 onwards, later to be joined by *Indefatigable* and *Implacable*. Escort carrier squadrons supported the assault on the South of France, Operation *Dragoon*, in August 1944, followed by a period of service in the Aegean. Nor were Seafires restricted to the European theatre; No 889 Squadron in *Atheling* began a short period of operations in the Indian Ocean in May 1944 and in November, the fleet carrier *Indefatigable* joined the Eastern Fleet

The end of the Seafire line was the Mk 47, VP485 being shown. This variant had a contra-prop as a standard feature (Mike Bowyer).

with 887 and 894 Seafire squadrons. They were followed by the escort carriers *Hunter* and *Stalker* and fleet carrier *Implacable*. The two big carriers were involved in the attacks on the Japanese islands with the US 3rd Fleet during July and August 1945. *Implacable* did not return to the UK until June 1946, when the last Merlin Seafire first-line unit, No 801 Squadron, disbanded.

Naturally enough, the Griffon-engined Spitfire led to the development of a Griffon-engined Seafire. In March 1943, Lieutenant-Commander E. M. Brown deck-landed a Spitfire XII on *Indomitable* to begin a series of trials to gain data for the development of a new breed of Seafire. A specification was drawn up for the naval fighter, N.4/43, and the designation Seafire XV was allocated. This does not mean that 11 unbuilt Seafire marks intervened between the L III and the Mark XV, the new mark number followed the Spitfire XIV. The new Seafire used the basic L III airframe with the addition of the fin and rudder of the Spitfire VIII and a retractable tail-wheel. The Griffon engine introduced a longer nose and the distinctive rocker box fairings on the upper cowling. Another new feature was the tail down position in catapult launching which did away with the need for catapult spools, substituting a

single hook under the centre section and a holdback point at the tail.

During production several further changes were to be made, most notably the installation of a 'sting' type arrester hook beneath the tail and the reduction in depth of the rear fuselage allowing a bubble canopy to be fitted. The latter provided the pilot with a much improved all-round view. Further alterations appeared in the Seafire XVII which introduced a new, stronger, long-stroke under-carriage which would stand up better to a heavy landing and help reduce bounce, which, in the earlier marks, tended to cause the aircraft to miss the arrester cables and sail into the crash barrier. It also had more fuel, giving a bit more endurance, provision for two fuselage-mounted reconnaissance cameras and underwing pick-up points for two 22.5-gallon slipper tanks or two 250 lb bombs or a further four 60 lb rocket projectiles.

The Mark XV entered service with three squadrons during 1946 and embarked in *Venerable, Ocean* and *Glory*. A fourth squadron, No 804, also received Mk XVs and joined *Theseus* in 1947. The Mark XVII served, shore based, with 807 Squadron and at sea with 800 Squadron in *Triumph*.

Specification N.7/44 brought about the final stage of development of the naval Spitfire. Based on the Spitfire Mk 21, the new Seafire Mk 45 had the two-stage Griffon 61 engine and a completely new wing. Although a production batch was built,

neither this nor the following Mk 46 were to be flown operationally from aircraft carriers. The Mk 46 introduced twin three-blade contra-rotating propellers which eliminated swing due to engine torque, greatly easing carrier take-off and landing. The definitive Seafire was the Mk 47 with the Griffon 88 engine with fuel injection, hydraulic wing folding and large vertical tail surfaces. The wing fold was different from earlier Seafires. Originally the position of the break was on the outer edge of the wheel wells, with a separately folding tip to reduce overall height. In the final versions there was a single fold outboard of the cannon bays.

Only two squadrons operated in the carrier-borne role with the Seafire Mk 47, No 800 in *Triumph* and No 804 in *Ocean*. The former, which formed on the type in February 1948, was in action against Communist terrorists in Malaya in October 1949, flying from the shore base at Sembawang. The following year, *Triumph* was involved in the Korean conflict, the Seafires of 800 Squadron being in action from July to September and seeing such hard use that when the carrier withdrew to Hong Kong, only one machine was fully serviceable. *Triumph* returned home in November 1950, 800 Squadron disbanded and there ended the seagoing life of the Seafire. Shore-based reserve and training units carried on with Seafires until the last disbandment in 1954.

Supermarine Seafire L III: *Span* 36 ft 10 in; *Length* 30 ft 2½ in; *Height* 11 ft 5½ in; *Wing area* 242 sq ft; *Engine* One 1,585 hp Rolls-Royce Merlin 55M; *All up weight* 7,640 lb; *Maximum speed* 348 mph at 6,000 ft; *Service ceiling* 24,000 ft; *Range* 513 miles (with 90 gallon drop tank); *Armament* 4 × 0.303 in Browning machine-guns and 2 × 20 mm Hispano cannon in the wings plus 1 × 500 lb bomb or 4 × 60 lb rocket projectiles.

Supermarine Seafire Mk 47: *Span* 36 ft 11 in (19 ft 1 in folded); *Length* 34 ft 4 in; *Height* 12 ft 9 in; *Wing area* 243.6 sq ft; *Engine* One 2,350 hp Rolls-Royce Griffon 88; *All up weight* 12,530 lb; *Maximum speed* 452 mph at 20,500 ft; *Service ceiling* 43,100 ft; *Range* 940 miles (with slipper tanks plus 90 gallon drop tank); *Armament* 4 × 20 mm British Hispano cannon in the wings, 8 × 60 lb rocket projectiles or 3 × 500 lb bombs.

Fairey Barracuda

Long before the first Fairey Albacore had flown, specification S.24/37 was issued for a monoplane torpedo-bomber-reconnaissance aircraft to replace it. The successful contender for this requirement was the Fairey Type 100, later to be officially named Barracuda. Power was to be from the ubiquitous Merlin, after schemes had been prepared around the Rolls-Royce Exe engine, development of which was discontinued at an early stage. Design was somewhat delayed by more urgent work on the Fulmar fighter, with the result that the first prototype did not make its maiden flight until December 7 1940. In its initial form, the prototype featured a low-mounted tailplane, but it was soon discovered that this suffered from severe buffeting caused by turbulence from the Fairey-Youngman flap/dive brakes beneath the inboard trailing edges of the mainplane. A redesigned empennage featured a high-mounted tailplane supported by struts rising from the rear fuselage. This solved the problem and was adopted for all production aircraft. The first prototype carried out a short series of initial deck-landing trials in *Victorious* in May 1941 before the new tail was fitted and the second prototype, complete with modified tail, took to the air on June 19.

The first production variant, the Barracuda I, was to reach a total of only 35 built before a change of engine from the Merlin 30 to the Merlin 32 introduced the Mark II, which became the standard production version. The first Barracuda I flew on May 18 1942 but it was not until January 1943 that No 827 Squadron began to re-equip from Albacores at Stretton. One reason for the delay was that several Barracudas had been lost when their wings came off in dives. This was traced to sub-standard wing locking pins causing wear which allowed a fatal lack of rigidity in the outspread wings.

The former Swordfish squadron, No 810, was the second unit to receive Barracudas, in April 1943, and the first to embark in a carrier for working up. This took place in June aboard *Illustrious*. Pairs of squadrons were formed into TBR Wings (Torpedo-Bomber-Reconnaissance) allocated to specific carriers and the 8th TBR Wing in *Furious*, with 827 and 830 Squadrons, was the first to see action. Off the Norwegian coast, in February 1944, attacks were made on enemy merchant shipping in the Leads. Two months later began the Barracuda's best known campaign—the *Tirpitz* attacks. The first series, under the codename of Operation *Tungsten*, began on April 3 and succeeded in inflicting severe damage on the *Tirpitz*, which had just completed repairs after previous damage received in the

Above *The first production Fairey Barracuda Mk 1, P9642, built at Heaton Chapel* (Imperial War Museum).

Left P9655 *in flight displays the shoulder wing of the Barracuda and the braced high-set tailplane.*

Below P9647 *was converted into the prototype Barracuda Mk II, the main wartime production version. Beneath the fuselage it carries a mine, the wing racks being available for smaller stores. A slight kink in the wing leading edge occurred because, when the undercarriage retracted, additional housing had to be added to the wing leading edge!* (Imperial War Museum).

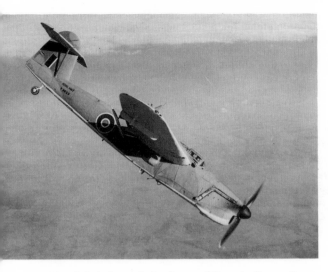

Although it had torpedo bomber capability, the Barracuda was equally intended as a dive bomber. P9659 *shown was a Mk 1.*

midget submarine attacks. The 21st TBR Wing, comprising 810 and 847 Squadrons in *Illustrious* was the first to take the Barracuda into action in the Far East, with an attack on the oil storage and port installations at Sabang on April 19 1944.

Several Barracudas were fitted with the ASV Mk IIN air-to-surface vessel radar for use against submarines. When the more effective ASV Mk X was fitted in a radome under the aft fuselage, the designation changed to Barracuda III. A few Mark IIs were also fitted with the American pod-mounted ASH (Air-to-Surface Homing) radar towards the war's end. As with its predecessors, the Swordfish and Albacore, the Barracuda flew from shore bases in attacks on enemy shipping, usually under the control of RAF Coastal Command, and scored some successes against German midget submarines operating off the Dutch coast in the last few weeks of the war. In the Pacific theatre, the 11th Aircraft Carrier Squadron, formed of the four new light fleet carriers *Colossus, Glory, Venerable* and *Vengeance*, was working up in Australian waters for the final assault on Japan, when the dropping of the atomic bombs brought an end to hostilities. These carriers' complements of Barracudas did not long survive the end of the war and the type began to be replaced by the Firefly. Shore-based Barracudas served for some years more including the final variant, the Griffon-engined Mk V, but the type's carrier-borne career was over with the exception of No 815 Squadron which re-formed in 1947 on Barracuda IIIs at Eglinton in the anti-submarine role and embarked in *Illustrious* for exercises.

Fairey Barracuda II: *Span* 49 ft 2½ in (18 ft 3 in folded); *Length* 39 ft 11½ in; *Height* 15 ft 0½ in; *Wing area* 405 sq ft; *Engine* One 1,640 hp Rolls-Royce Merlin 32; *All up weight* 14,080 lb; *Maximum speed* 228 mph at 1,750 ft; *Service ceiling* 16,600 ft; *Range* 524 miles (1,150 with maximum fuel and no bomb load); *Armament* 2 × 0.303 in Vickers K machine-guns in rear cockpit, 1 × 18 in torpedo or 6 × 250 lb bombs or 3 × 500 lb bombs or 4 × 285 lb Mk XI depth charges or 4 × 450 lb Mk VII depth charges.

Grumman Avenger

When the Grumman TBF-1 first joined the Fleet Air Arm in 1943 it was known as the Tarpon. The first squadron to form was No 832, whose personnel had sailed for America in December 1942 aboard *Victorious* in order to commence training on the new torpedo-bomber at the US Naval Air Station at Norfolk, Virginia. To begin with, this unit was equipped with US Navy aircraft, as the first of the batch of British machines was not available in time. Not only that, but their first embarkation was in the USS *Saratoga* which left for the Pacific theatre in April 1943. In May, No 832 rejoined *Victorious* for a period of operations in the Solomons.

Tarpon I was the designation given to the Grumman-built TBF-1, 1B or 1C variants until January 1944, when the name was officially changed to the original American one of Avenger, the British aircraft thenceforward being known as Avenger Is. The later marks were supplied from batches built by the Eastern Aircraft Division of

A Grumman Avenger Mk 1. Originally the type was called the Tarpon.

An Avenger 1, FN871, wearing an unusual paint scheme. For operations under Coastal Command its under surfaces are white, while the nose is black to aid in night attacks on shipping (Imperial War Museum).

General Motors who took over production from Grumman when priority was given to development of the new Hellcat fighter. The Eastern models were the TBM-1 and 1C which became the Fleet Air Arm's Avenger II and the TBM-3 and 3C which entered service as the Avenger III.

Of the Royal Navy's first-line units which operated Avengers during the war, the majority was formed and trained at the US East Coast bases at Norfolk, Quonset and Squantum. Deck-landing trials were made aboard USS *Charger*, which was one of the batch of RN escort carriers retained in America specifically for training duties. The fully trained and equipped squadrons would then be ferried to the British Isles in escort carriers to be operationally deployed. The Avengers were to be used in all the main theatres of war except for the Mediterranean and in several roles.

In 1953 the Fleet Air Arm again received Avengers, like XB391, for anti-submarine operations whilst the Gannet was developed (Mike Bowyer).

Despite provision for dropping the American 22.4 in torpedo, this weapon was not used in FAA Avengers owing to its poor performance compared to the British 18 in model carried by the Barracuda. Instead, it concentrated on a shallow dive attack, armed with either four 500 lb bombs or eight rocket projectiles. It could also carry mines or depth charges.

With the latter weapon, Avengers of 846 Squadron shared in the destruction of two German submarines. Embarked in the escort carrier *Tracker* covering convoys to Russia, they first sank *U.355* on April 1 1944 shared with the destroyer *Beagle* and then, on April 3, *U.288* was sunk in a combined attack with Swordfish from *Activity*'s 819 Squadron. Minelaying operations were also mounted from escort carriers to add an unknown quantity to the Norwegian coastal shipping lanes. Escort carriers operating in the Indian Ocean with Avengers claimed another submarine when *U.198* was attacked on August 12 1944 in concert with surface vessels. As already mentioned, *Victorious* had operated in the Solomons with 832 Squadron and this was the beginning of the Fleet Air Arm's highly active career in the Pacific theatre, notable in which were the bombing attacks on shore installations, in particular on the Japanese-held oil refineries on Java and Sumatra. As the tide of war swept inexorably, island by island, nearer to Japan itself, the Avenger was never far from the forefront of the action and was in action right up to August 15 1945, when Avengers from *Indefatigable*'s No 820 Squadron made bombing attacks on the environs of Tokyo.

Needless to say, the Avenger soon disappeared from first-line units of the Fleet Air Arm after the end of hostilities. But in 1953, an unexpected return to service came about when an anti-submarine aircraft was needed to fill the gap until the Fairey Gannet was ready. Under the Mutual Defense Assistance Program, Britain received 100 US standard TBM-3Es, the first arriving in March 1953. No 815 Squadron was first to equip in May, the Avengers replacing that unit's shore-based Barracudas. Conversion work undertaken by Scottish Aviation Ltd at Prestwick produced the AS Mk 4 and 5, equipped to British standards. These first entered service in 1954. When Gannets began to enter first line duty in 1955, the Avengers were gradually phased out and handed over to squadrons of the Royal Naval Volunteer Reserve.

Grumman Avenger I: *Span* 54 ft 2 in (19 ft 0 in folded); *Length* 40 ft 9 in; *Height* 13 ft 9 in; *Wing area* 490 sq ft; *Engine* One 1,700 hp Wright R-2600-8 Cyclone 14; *All up weight* 16,425 lbs; *Maximum speed* 257 mph at 12,000 ft; *Service ceiling* 21,400 ft; *Range* 1,105 miles; *Armament* 2 × 0.50 in Browning machine-guns in the wings, 1 × 0.50 in Browning machine-gun in the dorsal turret and 1 × 0.30 in Browning machine-gun in ventral position, 4 × 500 lb bombs or 8 × 60 lb rocket projectiles or depth charge or mines.

Vought Corsair

Such was the need to expand the Fleet Air Arm's fighter complement that when, in 1943, supplies of the Vought Corsair were made available under lend-lease, squadrons were formed and put aboard aircraft carriers despite the US Navy's not having cleared the type for operation from its own 'flat-tops'.

Dating back to a 1938 requirement, the prototype XF4U-1 had made its maiden flight on May 29 1940. Problems were encountered from the beginning, largely due to the combination of an untried powerplant (the Pratt & Whitney XR-2800-4 Double Wasp) and an airframe including several untried features. Apart from these problems, the most serious of which were due to the very high speeds (500 mph plus) attained in the vertical dive specified to be maintained for 10,000 ft and in recovery difficulties in spinning tests, US Navy pilots expressed concern over poor low speed characteristics and lack of forward visibility, both of which were instrumental in the aircraft's non-acceptance for carrier operations. However, the need to get high performance aircraft into the Pacific theatre of operations as soon as possible led to delivery priority being switched to Marine Corps squadrons for flying from shore bases. The first of these was formed in September 1942 and despatched to the Pacific at the turn of the year to support US forces on Guadalcanal where operations began in February 1943.

As for the Royal Navy, the Corsair's drawbacks in landing characteristics were accepted and squadrons began forming at the American bases at Quonset and Brunswick. They were, as with previous American types, ferried to Britain in escort carriers for operational allocations. The first Fleet Air Arm unit to form was No 1830 Squadron at Quonset on June 1 1943 and it was allocated to *Illustrious* on arrival in the UK. The first marks in the Royal Navy were the Corsair I and II, both being the Vought F4U-1 variant with the distinguishing feature being the earlier metal reinforced canopy in the former and the improved clear-view plexiglas canopy in the latter. The designations Corsair III and IV went to the F3A-1

Opposite page *The Vought Corsair had a number of unusual features, among them the inverted gull wing and retracting undercarriage of peculiar geometry* (F.C. Dickey).

Right *A Corsair II (F4U-1D), JT565, wearing markings applicable to naval aircraft operated in the Far East* (Christopher Hak).

and FG-1 respectively. Both these marks were equivalent to the F4U-1 but built under licence by Brewster and Goodyear. A unique distinguishing feature of FAA Corsairs was the removal of 8 in from each wingtip to reduce the folded height of the aircraft to allow their accommodation in the hangars of escort carriers. The operational debut of the British Corsair was on April 3 1944 when aircraft of *Victorious'* 1834 Squadron flew as an element of the fighter cover for the attacks by Barracudas on the *Tirpitz* (Operation *Tungsten*). On April 19, 1830 and 1833 Squadrons in *Illustrious* supported Barracudas attacking Sabang in Sumatra. In July and August 1944 Corsairs were again involved in the strikes against *Tirpitz*, flying from *Formidable*.

The Corsair's greatest honour in Fleet Air Arm service was achieved as the mount of Lieutenant Robert Hampton Gray of the Royal Canadian Naval Volunteer Reserve. Flying with *Formidable's* No 1841 Squadron on August 9 1945, Gray led an attack on Japanese naval units in the waters of Onagawa Wan on the north-east coast of Honshu. Flying Corsair IV, *KD658*, he pressed home his attack through the intense anti-aircraft barrage, achieving hits with his two 500 lb bombs on the escort vessel *Amakusa*. The ship quickly sank. However, Gray's Corsair was hit during the attack and plunged in flames into the bay. His courage was recognized by the posthumous award of a Victoria

Cross, the only carrier pilot to be so honoured.

Vought Corsair II: *Span* 39 ft $7\frac{3}{4}$ in (clipped wings, 17 ft $0\frac{5}{8}$ in folded); *Length* 32 ft $9\frac{1}{2}$ in; *Height* 15 ft $0\frac{1}{4}$ in; *Wing area* 305 sq ft (clipped wings); *Engine* One 2,000 hp Pratt & Whitney R-2800-8 Double Wasp; *All up weight* 13,846 lb; *Maximum speed* 392 mph at 24,000 ft; *Service ceiling* 37,100 ft; *Range* 1,070 miles; *Armament* 6 × 0.50 in Colt-Browning machine-guns and 2 × 1,000 lb or 2 × 500 lb bombs.

Grumman Hellcat

Development problems with the Vought Corsair prompted the US Navy to order a further aircraft as insurance, should the Corsair prove a failure. A contract was placed with Grumman in June 1941 for two prototypes of what was originally considered to be an improved F4F (Wildcat). As development proceeded the aircraft emerged as a completely new fighter—the F6F Hellcat.

Hellcats entered US Navy service in January 1943 and in the summer of that year the first of a batch of F6F-3s began to arrive in Britain where they entered the Fleet Air Arm as Hellcat F Is. The first squadron to commission was No 800 at Eglinton, closely followed by No 804 at the same

Above left *Grumman Hellcat 1s ranged upon a carrier* en route *to the Far East.*

Left *An early Hellcat Mk 1, FN437.*

Above JV105, *a Hellcat 1 aboard a carrier off Algeria.*

Below *Action stations among the Hellcats during operations in the Pacific in 1945.*

Grumman Hellcat IIs in overall dark blue finish (Burgess).

base. Intensive flying training was carried out during August and September, including a series of ADDLs (Aerodrome Dummy Deck Landings), leading up to deck landing trials aboard *Ravager* in the Clyde in October. At the end of 1943, both squadrons were allocated to the escort carrier *Emperor* and their first operation was to cover a Gibraltar convoy in February 1944.

Hellcats were involved in the three major operations against the battleship *Tirpitz* in Norwegian waters, initially with *Emperor*'s two squadrons in the *Tungsten* strikes in April and in Operations *Mascot* and *Goodwood* in July and August, with No 1840 Squadron in *Furious* and *Indefatigable*. The August 1944 invasion of the South of France saw *Emperor* operating in support, her Hellcat squadrons having merged under the number of 800. In September, with the squadron operating as part of the 7th Naval fighter Wing, the carrier was in the waters of the Aegean.

The arrival of F6F-5s and 5Ns brought to the Royal Navy the Hellcat Mark II in several sub-variants. The basic fighter was known simply as the F Mk II; with the addition of a reconnaissance camera this became FR Mk II and with the camera but without the wing guns, PR Mk II. The F6F-5N was a night fighter equipped with AN/APS-6 radar in a pod beneath the outer starboard wing and was designated NF Mk II. Two squadrons were working

up on the night fighter when the war ended, and, consequently, they did not see action. Hellcats served with eight squadrons in the Indian and Pacific Oceans from the end of 1944. Most were embarked in escort carriers but *Indomitable*'s 5th Naval Fighter Wing comprised Nos 1839 and 1844 Squadrons with Hellcats. These went into action against Japanese targets in Sumatra, the Sakishima Gunto and Formosa as the Allies swept back across the Pacific. A vital element of the campaign in that ocean was the Fleet Train of supply ships, carrying ammunition, replacement aircraft, fuel, spares and food. No 1840 Squadron Hellcats in *Speaker* were allocated as air defence for those precious ships.

With the war over, the Hellcat quickly disappeared from the Fleet Air Arm, only two units remaining till 1946, and the majority of the remaining airworthy aircraft were returned to the United States under the terms of the lend-lease agreement.

Grumman Hellcat I: *Span* 42 ft 10 in (16 ft 2 in folded); *Length* 33 ft 4 in; *Height* 14 ft 5 in; *Wing area* 334 sq ft; *Engine* One 2,000 hp Pratt & Whitney R-2800-10 Double Wasp; *All up weight* 13,221 lb; *Maximum speed* 373 mph at 23,700 ft; *Service ceiling* 37,500 ft; *Range* 1,620 miles (with drop tank); *Armament* 6 × 0.50 in Colt-Browning machine-guns.

Above *Part of a post-war carrier force, Firefly 1s are escorted by Seafire F XVs all operating from HMS Theseus.*

Right *To assist in naval observer/radar operator training, a number of Firefly 1s were converted, after the war, into T Mk 3s including PP435 (Mike Bowyer).*

Fairey Firefly

The Fulmar had been created in a hurry as a carrier-borne fighter in order to close the gap between the high performance land-based aircraft of the Royal Air Force and the current Fleet Air Arm equipment, the Sea Gladiator and Skua. The Admiralty quickly followed up with a requirement for a two-seat fighter-reconnaissance aircraft of more advanced performance. Two specifications were issued, one of which, N.9/39, called for a turret-armed fighter which was mercifully not proceeded with. As the performance of the Blackburn Roc and the unfortunate experience of the RAF's Defiant during the Battle of Britain showed,

the turret fighter was a vulnerable and unwieldy aircraft in a dog-fight. The Fairey team, under H. E. Chaplin, based its design on the N.8/39 requirement and a mock-up of this proposal was accepted for production on June 6 1940. A new covering specification, N.5/40, was drawn up and a contract placed for 200 aircraft off the drawing board. No prototypes were built as such but the first three of the batch were constructed by hand in the experimental shop at Hayes, for use as development aircraft.

The first flight was made on December 22 1941 by C. S. Staniland from the Great West Aerodrome, Heathrow. The fifth aircraft built was the first to be delivered to the Navy on March 4 1943. Designated

Firefly I, the aeroplane was powered by the Rolls-Royce Griffon IIB, had an armament of four 20 mm Hispano cannon and featured the Fairey-Youngman area-increasing flaps. These flaps, in addition to the normal function of such items, extended aft on tracks to give an increase in wing area for cruising flight and were instrumental in giving the Firefly its agility which was so vital an attribute in combat.

The fourth Firefly had carried out initial carrier trials in *Illustrious* towards the end of 1942. To begin the type's service career, 12 aircraft were allotted to No 1770 Squadron, which formed at Yeovilton on October 1 1943. After operating from the shore bases of Grimsetter and Hatston, the squadron embarked in the new aircraft carrier *Indefatigable* prior to the mounting of Operation *Mascot* in July 1944. This attempt on the *Tirpitz*, lurking in Norway's Altenfjord, was not successful due mainly to poor visibility occasioned by the smoke apparatus

set up around the ship's anchorage and by fog. The Fireflies' most important contribution to the *Tirpitz* affair was to carry out reconnaissance flights over the fjord and the information gleaned on these sorties was put to good use in the attacks made by the Lancasters of Nos 9 and 617 Squadrons which finally destroyed the ship in November 1944.

The development history of further wartime marks of Firefly is somewhat convoluted. Put simply, a proposed night fighter version, designated NF Mk II with AI Mk X radar in wing-mounted radomes, was suppressed when a more compact canister-mounted radar was produced which could be carried beneath the forward fuselage of the standard Mark I. Ultimately, with the ASH radar fit available, two sub-variants were produced, the FR Mk I and the NF Mk I. These were basically similar except that the latter had shrouded exhausts or a flame shield above the exhaust stubs to prevent the pilot's night vision being impaired. Re-engining with the Griffon 61, which would have introduced the Firefly III, was abandoned when the prototype was found to be aerodynamically unstable. Instead a redesign was initiated which was to result in the Mark IV.

After the Firefly's brief combat initiation in Norwegian waters, in which it had not had a chance to engage in fighter-to-fighter conflict, its scene of action moved to the Indian and Pacific Oceans for

Left *An early production Firefly IV approaches a carrier deck.*

Below left *Firefly AS 5 VX413, the last built with manually folded wings, taxies by at Ford in July 1955* (Mike Bowyer).

Below *The final Firefly in the series with conventional engine layout was the anti-submarine Mk 6, WD918 being depicted here.*

the final year of the war. Here it was to prove its effectiveness, both in air-to-air combat with Japanese aircraft and in the ground attack role equipped with loads of eight rockets or pairs of 500 or 1,000 lb bombs. By the end of the war, in August 1945, four fully equipped squadrons had seen action, flying from the carriers *Indefatigable* and *Implacable.* To the Firefly fell the honour of being the first British aircraft to fly over Tokyo during the attacks on the Japanese home islands. An additional display of the type's capability had been shown in tests at the US Navy's Patuxent River establishment, where a Firefly on evaluation had consistently bested a Grumman Hellcat in mock combat interception.

Development of the Firefly IV proceeded throughout 1944–45 using four Mark I airframes, including that previously flown as the Mark III. The production aircraft, of which the first flew on May 25 1945, was powered by the Griffon 74, the torque from this more powerful engine demanding a larger fin and rudder to maintain directional control. Radar was installed in a radome beneath the starboard wing and a similarly shaped fuel tank was fitted to the port wing to preserve symmetry. As with the Mark I, two sub-variants were produced, the FR Mk IV and the NF Mk IV. With the war over, production was less urgent and it was not until September 1946 that the first Mark IV was delivered to the Navy. In the meantime, Mark Is were still being distributed

to the squadrons. In 1946, the Netherlands placed an order for Fireflies of both marks, the Mark Is equipping two squadrons aboard *Karel Doorman* (ex-*Venerable* handed over in 1948). Towards the end of 1947 No 825 Squadron became the first to equip with the Firefly IV at Eglinton. The squadron had been transferred on loan to the Royal Canadian Navy in 1946 for service aboard the carrier *Warrior.* The fifty mark of Firefly, which was distinguished by variation in equipment installed, introduced a new leading role—that of anti-submarine warfare. Under the designation AS Mk 5 this, together with the FR Mk 5 and NF Mk 5, began to enter service in January 1948, firstly with No 814 Squadron at Yeovilton. Mark 5s were allocated to 825 Squadron in *Magnificent* and two squadrons, Nos 816 and 817 equipped with Marks 4 and 5 and the specialist AS Mk 6, were detached to the Royal Australian Navy with which they served in *Sydney* (ex-*Terrible*).

The Korean War which erupted in 1950 was to see much use of carrier-borne aircraft and the Firefly was one of the types in the forefront of the

Below *A tall fin and rudder compensated for the unusual radiator layout on the Firefly AS 7* (Mike Bowyer).

Right *Luckily the Firefly AS 5 has not entirely vanished from view, as proven by this illustration of* WB271 *at the 1981 Mildenhall Air Fete* (Mike Bowyer).

action. The first of the six squadrons to be involved was 827 in *Triumph* and the Firefly's chief contribution was to give close support to the land forces, carrying up to 2,000 lb of bombs and rockets per sortie. As many as 123 sorties in one day were mounted by the Sea Fury and the Firefly, this record being set by 802 and 825 Squadrons in *Ocean* on May 17 1952.

As already mentioned, the AS Mk 6 was a dedicated anti-submarine aircraft, having the four Hispano cannon deleted and being equipped with sonobuoys and associated receivers for the detection of submarines. The AS Mk 5 carried American, and the AS Mk 6 British, sonobuoy equipment. By the end of 1951, when all Firefly 6s had been delivered, development was under way of the Fairey Gannet anti-submarine aircraft which was intended to replace the Firefly in service. But problems over this newcomer meant that there would be a delay in its introduction and this brought about the appearance of another, final, variant of the anti-sub Firefly as an interim solution. Work on this, the AS Mk 7, was started in 1949 and a prototype was in the air in May 1951. Fitted with the Griffon 59 engine

and a further redesigned fin and rudder, the AS Mk 7 also had a third crew member in the aft cockpit to help reduce the workload of the single observer of earlier marks. In the event, only one front line squadron, No 824, was equipped with this mark owing to the availability of Grumman Avengers under the Mutual Defense Assistance Program from America. This spelt the end for the Firefly as a front line aircraft although many would soldier on for years in training, target drone and target-towing roles.

Fairey Firefly I: *Span* 44 ft 6 in (13 ft 6 in folded); *Length* 37 ft 7 in; *Height* 13 ft 7 in; *Wing area* 328 sq ft; *Engine* One 1,735 hp Rolls-Royce Griffon IIB; *All up weight* 14,288 lb; *Maximum speed* 319 mph at 17,000 ft; *Service ceiling* 29,000 ft; *Range* 774 miles; *Armament* 4 × 20 mm Hispano cannon and 8 × 60 lb rocket projectiles or 2 × 500 lb or 2 × 1,000 lb bombs.
Fairey Firefly FR Mk IV: *Span* 41 ft 2 in (13 ft 6 in folded); *Length* 38 ft 0 in; *Height* 13 ft 11 in; *Wing area* 330 sq ft; *Engine* One 2,190 hp Rolls-Royce Griffon 74; *All up weight* 15,600 lb; *Maximum speed* 345 mph

at 12,500 ft; *Service ceiling* 29,200 ft; *Range* 582 miles; *Armament* 4 × 20 mm Hispano cannon and 8 × 60 lb rocket projectiles or 2 × 500 lb or 2 × 1,000 lb bombs or 2 × 1,000 lb mines.

Fairey Firefly AS Mk 7: *Span* 44 ft 6 in (13 ft 6 in folded); *Length* 38 ft 3 in; *Height* 13 ft 3 in; *Wing area* 342 sq ft; *Engine* One 1,965 hp Rolls-Royce Griffon 59; *All up weight* 13,970 lb; *Maximum speed* 300 mph at 10,750 ft; *Service ceiling* 25,500 ft; *Range* 860 miles; *Armament* No offensive armament carried.

Blackburn Firebrand

The first stage in the development of the Firebrand torpedo-fighter was the Blackburn B.37 to specification N.11/40, drawn up as a single-seat fleet fighter by chief designer George Petty in July 1940. With an armament of four wing-mounted 20 mm Hispano cannon, the B.37 was to be powered by the Napier Sabre III 24-cylinder in-line 'H' layout engine. The first prototype was complete and ready to fly in January 1942. After engine tests and taxiing trials had been completed the aircraft was towed from Brough to Leconfield by road for its maiden flight, which was made by Flight Lieutenant Arthur Thompson on February 27 1942. The second and third prototypes were flying by September and the second prototype, with its Hispano cannon installed, was delivered to the Naval Air Station at Machrihanish in October,

beginning carrier trials in *Illustrious* in February 1943.

Back at Brough, a crash landing due to engine seizure from a burst oil pipe put the second prototype out of action for some time and during rebuilding the aircraft was transformed into the TF Mk II, with a strengthened under-fuselage position for a 1,850 lb 18 in torpedo. When 24 Sabre-powered Firebrands had been completed (including the three prototypes) a decision by the Ministry of Aircraft Production to allocate all the Sabre engines to Hawker for the Typhoon, meant a redesign of the Blackburn aircraft to take the Bristol Centaurus VII 18-cylinder two-row radial. The new Blackburn type number B.45 was allotted and production as the Firebrand TF Mk III, to specification S.8/43, ensued.

Much development work was needed to achieve successful torpedo drops owing to the greater speed of the Firebrand compared with current operational types such as the Swordfish and Albacore. If the 'fish' was dropped at too great a speed, it was liable to porpoise on entering the water or to break its back. Therefore airbrakes were designed and fitted to the top and bottom surfaces of the mainplane, near to the leading edge, to give a reduction in speed of about 70 mph. The torpedo was attached to

The Blackburn Firebrand was a large, noisy fighter. The Mk 1 shown, DD810, was the second Sabre-powered prototype and was photographed on July 30 1942 (Fairey).

Above DD810 *was subsequently incorporated in NV636, the prototype of a torpedo-carrying attack version of the Firebrand, the TF 2.*

Right *A Firebrand IV photographed at Brough, Yorkshire, its birthplace* (R.V.K. Jackson).

Below *General problems with the Sabre throughout its career led to the adoption of the Centaurus engine in the Firebrand TF 4, EK660 being illustrated.*

a two-position carrier, which, on the ground, held the weapon at 6 degrees nose down to allow ground clearance and, on retraction of the undercarriage, moved it up through 7 degrees to the dropping position. In addition, the torpedo was fitted with the Monoplane Air Tail Mk IV for directional stability in flight, which was released automatically as the torpedo entered the water.

Although half of the 12 Mk IIs were allocated to 708 Squadron at Lee-on-Solent during 1944 for service trials, the Firebrand was not to enter first-line duty until the war was over. The further developed TF Mk IV, which featured a larger fin and rudder, joined 813 Squadron at Ford in 1945, the unit having re-formed on September 1. Somewhat ironically, 813's Firebrands took part in the Victory Fly-past over London on June 8 1946. Before embarking in *Illustrious* in 1947, the squadron had re-equipped with the TF Mk V (Blackburn B.46) which had control refinements in the form of horn balanced elevators and long span aileron tabs. The only other carrier-borne squadron was No 827, which formed on the Firebrand TF Mk 5A at Ford in December 1950. The A suffix denoted the addition of hydraulically boosted ailerons, giving an increased rate of roll. Three years later, both squadrons relinquished their Firebrands prior to re-forming on the Westland Wyvern.

Blackburn Firebrand TF Mk 5: *Span* 51 ft $3\frac{1}{2}$ in (16 ft 1 in folded); *Length* 38 ft 9 in; *Height* 13 ft 3 in; *Wing area* 383 sq ft; *Engine* One 2,250 hp Bristol Centaurus IX; *All up weight* 16,700 lb; *Maximum speed* 350 mph at 13,000 ft; *Service ceiling* 31,000 ft; *Range* 745 miles; *Armament* 4 × 20 mm Hispano cannon and 1 × 18 ins torpedo plus 2 × 500 lb bombs or 6 × 60 lb rocket projectiles or 1 × 2,000 lb bomb in place of the torpedo.

de Havilland Sea Hornet

The de Havilland D.H.103 Hornet originated in 1942. Started as a private venture to develop a high-speed twin-engine fighter for use in the Pacific War, it was to use a new version of the Rolls-Royce Merlin. The new variant of this famous engine had a smaller frontal area than previous examples, allowing a much cleaner nacelle design. In addition, the engines were geared so that one propeller rotated in the opposite direction to the other, so eliminating the tendency to swing on take-off. A mock-up of the proposed aircraft was built and this was inspected by the Ministry of Aircraft Production. In June 1943, development was officially ordered to proceed, with specification F.12/43 written to cover it. The first prototype Hornet was completed by the middle of 1944 and a first flight made by Geoffrey de Havilland on July 28 1944. Thereafter work proceeded to get the aircraft into Royal Air Force service.

Quite early on in the development programme, the company was aware that the Hornet held great potential as a high performance carrier-borne fighter, again with an eye on the Pacific War. The lack of swing due to opposite rotation of the propellers would be of great benefit in carrier take-offs and landings. Towards the end of 1944, a new specification, N.5/44, was drafted to cover separate development as the aircraft that would become the Sea Hornet. Three Hornet airframes were transferred to the Heston Aircraft Company, which was given responsibility for design of the naval aircraft

The first naval version of the Hornet, the de Havilland Sea Hornet F 20—VR892 shown (Dave Menard).

With very prominent nose radome, a Sea Hornet NF 21 taxies out at the 1953 Naval Coronation Review (Mike Bowyer).

to ease the workload on the de Havilland team. Naval features had to be worked into the design and the three Hornets were to be modified to varying degrees as Sea Hornet prototypes.

The first was completed without folding wings to save time and made its first flight from Heston on April 19 1945. Initial carrier trials followed in *Ocean*, starting with the first deck landing on August 10 1945, the day that the Pacific War ended. Nevertheless, development proceeded, to give the Navy its first post-war fighter in the form of the Sea Hornet F Mk 20, a batch of 80 being ordered from the parent firm with the production line being set up at Hatfield. The first of these took to the air on August 13 1946. Deliveries started in October to No 703 Squadron at Lee-on-Solent to begin service trials and the following year No 801 Squadron re-formed on Sea Hornets at Ford on June 1. In October 1948 another series of trials was carried out in *Illustrious* to prove a redesigned undercarriage.

No 801, after a working up period at Arbroath, embarked in *Implacable* in 1949 for the type's first seagoing commission. As it turned out, this was to be the only carrier-borne squadron to equip with the Mark 20, as continued development and changing requirements brought a change of role to that of night fighter. The Heston design team, working to specification N.21/45, designed a nose-mounted radome to contain ASH radar equipment and a

second cockpit sited in line with the trailing edge of the wing to house the radar operator/observer. A standard Hornet airframe was allotted to carry out trials of different radome shapes, making its first flight on July 9 1946. The first production Sea Hornet NF Mk 21 flew on March 24 1948 and deck trials began in *Illustrious* on October 25, including a series of night flying trials.

The Naval Air Fighting Development Unit and Service Trials Unit based at Ford carried out service testing of the type and on January 20 1949 No 809 Squadron formed on NF 21s, also at Ford. As with the Mark 20 there was to be only the one front line unit equipped with the night fighter. No 809 worked up at Culdrose, with deck landings in *Illustrious*, before embarking in *Vengeance* in May 1951. This lasted for a mere 12 days owing to the aircraft being found unsuitable for operation from the light fleet carriers. In June 1952 the squadron joined *Indomitable*, then transferred to *Eagle*, remaining with her until disbandment in 1954. One other mark built was the Sea Hornet PR Mk 22, which was an unarmed Mk 20 fitted with three reconnaissance cameras, including a night camera. None of these saw service in a carrier.

de Havilland Sea Hornet NF Mk 21: *Span* 45 ft 0 in (27 ft 6 in folded); *Length* 37 ft 0 in; *Height* 14 ft 2 in; *Wing area* 361 sq ft; *Engines* Two 2,030 hp Rolls-Royce Merlin 134/135; *All up weight* 19,530 lb; *Maximum speed* 430 mph at 22,000 ft; *Service ceiling* 36,500 ft; *Range* 1,500 miles; *Armament* 4 × 20 mm Hispano cannon in the nose plus 2 × 1,000 lb bombs or 8 × 60 lb rocket projectiles under wings.

Hawker Sea Fury

The Fleet Air Arm's final piston-engined shipboard fighter began to take shape in 1943 in response to specification N.7/43. The slightly earlier specification F.2/43 had been drafted to cover Hawker schemes for a smaller version of the Tempest for the Royal Air Force, and, at Sydney Camm's suggestion, a single basic design would be produced to meet both requirements, with detail refinements for land-based and naval variants. Power was to be supplied by the Bristol Centaurus and detail development of the naval model was entrusted to Boulton Paul Aircraft. In 1944, a production order was placed for 200 of each variant, in the case of the naval aircraft, to the revised specification N.22/43. The first machine to fly was the first prototype of the Fury, as the RAF fighter was to be known, on September 1 1944. The Boulton Paul Sea Fury prototype was not at such an advanced stage and was destined to be transferred to Hawker's Kingston factory for completion when the production contract for the Fury was cancelled and that for the Sea Fury reduced to the 100 ordered from the parent firm. This occurred in January 1945 and was

due to the favourable situation then attaining in the European War and the steady progress of jet aircraft development.

Two of the Fury prototypes were converted on the line to become Sea Fury prototypes and the first of these completed its maiden flight on February 21 1945. It was subsequently delivered to the RAE at Farnborough for trials, prior to carrier tests. Directional stability on take-off and landing caused some problems but by the beginning of August the aircraft was cleared for deck-landing trials. These commenced on August 10 1945 aboard *Ocean*, concurrently with those of the Sea Hornet. The fully navalised second prototype flew on October 12 1945 and the similarly equipped, former Boulton Paul third prototype followed on January 31 1946.

The first production Sea Fury Mk X took to the air on September 7 1946. In March 1947 catapult trials were carried out in *Illustrious* followed by intensive deck-landing trials in *Victorious*. The first operational squadron to equip was No 807 at Eglinton which replaced its Seafires in August 1947 and a further three first-line units formed on Sea Fury Mk Xs. After 50 of that mark had been built, production switched to the FB Mk 11 which, in

Rejected by the RAF as outdated by jet fighters, the Hawker Fury was eagerly accepted by the Royal Navy. VR932, an FB Mk II, is seen here in the early style of Service markings (Dave Menard).

This page *Sea Fury 11s served most usefully in the Korean War, and made a major contribution to the memorable 1953 Coronation Naval Review fly-past* (Mike Bowyer).

addition to many detail improvements, had an increased weapon load capability and provision for rocket assisted take-off gear (RATOG). No 802 Squadron was the first to receive the Mk 11 in May 1948, again at Eglinton, and they embarked in *Vengeance* in 1949. In 1950, 807 Squadron in *Theseus* took its Sea Furies into action in the Korean War,

the first sorties being flown on December 7. The type achieved great distinction in this conflict, numbering among its successes several of the potent MiG-15 jets destroyed in air-to-air encounters.

In 1953, the turbojet-powered Hawker Sea Hawk began to usurp the Sea Fury as the Royal Navy's leading single-seat fighter and in the following year all first-line units had been re-equipped. The FB 11s continued to serve through the mid-50s with RNVR units. Mention should be made of the Sea Fury T Mk 20 which first flew on January 15 1948 and which featured a second cockpit for the instructor aft of the wing trailing edge. T Mk 20s were issued to the first-line squadrons for instrument flying training.

Hawker Sea Fury FB Mk 11: *Span* 38 ft 4¾ in (16 ft 1 in folded); *Length* 34 ft 8 in; *Height* 15 ft 10½ in; *Wing area* 280 sq ft; *Engine* One 2,550 hp Bristol Centaurus 18; *All up weight* 14,650 lb; *Maximum speed* 460 mph at 18,000 ft; *Service ceiling* 35,800 ft; *Range* 700 miles; *Armament* 4 × 20 mm Hispano cannon plus 2 × 500 lb or 2 × 1,000 lb bombs or 12 × 60 lb rocket projectiles or 4 × 180 lb Triplex rockets.

Supermarine Attacker

In 1943, Joseph Smith, Supermarine's chief designer and successor to the famed R. J. Mitchell, drew up a design for a new fighter to specification F.1/43 as a successor to the Spitfire. The main element of this design was a new wing of laminar-flow section, in which the thickest part is much nearer the mid-chord position than usual. It also featured a wide-track, inward retracting undercarriage, which would greatly improve the stability of the aircraft while moving on the ground. The name bestowed on the new aeroplane was Spiteful.

However, by June 1944, when the Spiteful prototype flew, development of the jet engine had led Joe Smith to design a new aircraft, which he submitted as a private venture to the MAP. This, the Type 392 Jet Spiteful, consisted of a completely new but essentially simple fuselage with lateral air intakes to supply one of the new Rolls-Royce Nene turbojets with tail-emitting jet-pipe, combined with the laminar-flow wing of the Spiteful. The design was approved in mock-up form and specification E.10/44 issued to cover prototype development. The prototype Type 392 was taken to Boscombe Down in 1946 to carry out initial trials, the first flight being made on July 27 by Supermarine test pilot Jeffrey Quill.

Two further prototypes were completed to specification E.1/45. These were Type 398s with naval equipment to permit deck landing and were the true prototypes of the Attacker, which name was allotted early in 1947. The first flight of a Type 398 was

Like the Fury, the Supermarine Attacker was rejected by the RAF, to become the Navy's first operational carrier-based jet fighter. Late production examples served as fighter bombers, including the FB Mk 2 illustrated which was photographed at Benson (Mike Bowyer).

made at Chilbolton on June 17 1947 in the hands of Lieutenant-Commander Michael Lithgow. The following October saw initial deck landing trials in *Illustrious*. Despite the success of these trials, it was to be more than two years before an order for production was placed, as the Navy was at that time embroiled in the theory and practice of under-carriage-less deck-landing and a decision on which way development should go was delayed until the 'rubber deck' trials were completed in 1949.

The production Supermarine Attacker F Mk 1 was armed with four Hispano cannon in the wings, the outer panels of which folded upward for carrier stowage. The first aircraft flew on May 5 1950. The straight fighter became the FB Mk 1 with under-wing positions for bombs or rocket projectiles and the definitive FB Mk 2 standardised a forward extension of the fin, which had been added in retrospect to some Mark 1s, and had a metal-framed canopy. Deliveries of production aircraft began in January 1951 to the Naval Air Fighting

Development Unit at West Raynham and on August 17 No 800 Squadron at Ford became the first operational unit to equip with jet aircraft when it formed with eight Attackers. No 800 started its first embarkation in *Eagle* on March 4 1952, the new carrier having commissioned only on March 1. A second Attacker squadron, No 803, had been formed in November 1951 and a third, No 890, formed in April 1952. The latter soon relinquished its aircraft, which were then handed to 800 and 803 to increase their complements. Both squadrons were operated from *Eagle* and were destined to serve their entire first-line careers in that ship. By 1954 the Attacker was obsolete and the two squadrons were disbanded. The type saw a short period of service with second-line and reserve units before disappearing from the Fleet Air Arm for good.

Supermarine Attacker FB Mk 2: *Span* 36 ft 11 in (28 ft 11 in folded); *Length* 37 ft 1 in; *Height* 9 ft 6½ in; *Wing area* 227.2 sq ft; *Engine* One 5,100 lb st Rolls-Royce Nene 102; *All up weight* 12,300 lb; *Maximum speed* 590 mph at sea level; *Service ceiling* 45,000 ft; *Range* 590 miles (1,190 miles with overload tank); *Armament* 4 × 20 mm Hispano cannon and 2 × 1,000 lb bombs or 12 × 60 lb rocket projectiles.

Attacker FB 2 WK342 exhibits the manner by which the aircraft's wing tips could be folded.

Douglas Skyraider

Out of the Pacific War came the lesson that shipboard radar gave inadequate warning of the approach of low-flying aircraft, a point made abundantly clear by the high rate of hits registered by Japanese kamikaze aircraft. It was quickly realised that an effective answer to this problem would be to put long-range radar equipment into an aeroplane, which, on standing patrol, could give ample warning of attack.

As events were to unfold, the Second World War had ended before such an aircraft could be brought into service, but the Americans had produced a radar picket out of the Grumman Avenger before the close of hostilities and work was in hand to produce a follow-up from the new Douglas Destroyer II attack aircraft. This evolved into the AD-1 Skyraider and the first radar-equipped airborne early warning variant flew in prototype form as the XAD-1W in 1946. In 1950 the latest model on order for the US Navy was the AD-4W fitted with APS-20 radar and from the 168 production aircraft, 50 were to be transferred to Britain under the Mutual Defense Assistance Program, to serve as Skyraider AEW Mk 1s in the Fleet Air Arm.

The first four aircraft arrived by sea in November 1951 and were delivered to 778 Squadron at Culdrose for evaluation of the electronic equipment. Initial deck trials were carried out aboard *Eagle* in

The Royal Navy acquired Douglas Skyraider AEW 1s in the early '50s, the example shown serving aboard HMS Eagle *when photographed. Aged as they would now seem, the Skyraiders might well have had a useful part to play in the South Atlantic, with updated radar—and an attack carrier as their base (Mike Bowyer).*

February 1952. The following July, the four-aircraft-strong 778 was redesignated as the Headquarters Flight of No 849 Squadron, with further flights to be formed for carrier service as more Skyraiders were delivered. 'A' Flight was formed in January 1953 and embarked in *Eagle* at the end of the month. So began the Skyraider's Royal Navy career which was to last eight years, till the end of 1960, when 'D' Flight, then allocated to *Albion*, parted with its last example on conversion to the Fairey Gannet AEW 3. Both 'A' and 'C' Flights had been involved in Operation *Musketeer*, the Suez campaign of 1956, aboard *Eagle* and *Albion* respectively.

Douglas Skyraider AEW Mk 1: *Span* 50 ft $0\frac{1}{4}$ in (23 ft $10\frac{1}{2}$ in folded); *Length* 38 ft 10 in: *Height* 15 ft $7\frac{1}{2}$ in; *Wing area* 400 sq ft; *Engine* One 2,700 hp Wright R-3350-26WA Cyclone; *All up weight* 24,000 lb; *Maximum speed* 321 mph at sea level; *Service ceiling* 36,000 ft; *Range* 1,280 miles (with two 150 gallon drop tanks); *Armament* No offensive weapons carried.

It is not generally appreciated what a major role was envisaged for the Westland Wyvern. Planned as a long range intruder fighter bomber for the RAF, and powered by a Rolls-Royce Eagle, great things were demanded of it. The prototype shown here appeared too late for RAF interest to be sustained.

Westland Wyvern

In 1944 the design staff of Westland Aircraft Limited under the leadership of W. E. W. Petter, and, after his departure for English Electric, of Arthur Davenport, formulated outline proposals for a single-engine torpedo fighter and succeeded in obtaining the support of Rear Admiral Sir Matthew Slattery, Director General of Naval Aircraft Development and Production at the Ministry of Supply. Two basic design proposals were built in mock-up form for consideration by service and government experts and a conventional layout front-engined aeroplane was chosen over a more radical mid-engined version in which the propeller was to be driven by an extension shaft running beneath the cockpit. The official specification N.11/44 was drafted to cover the design, the development of which was to be under the firm's chief designer John Digby.

An attempt to gain the interest of the RAF in the

new aircraft was not to bear fruit. Six prototypes were ordered in November 1944 and choice of powerplant was directed to the Rolls-Royce Eagle 24-cylinder horizontal-H piston engine, though from early in the design stage consideration had been given to the use of a turbo-prop. Development of the turbojet was taking on a greater significance at this time and the Rolls-Royce Eagle was to be limited to a small production batch specifically for Westland's W.34, as the machine was designated. This necessitated an investigation into an alternative engine for the production aircraft and the specification N.12/45 was issued to cover a Mark 2 (W.35) version of which three prototypes were ordered in February 1946. Two of these would have Armstrong Siddeley Pythons and the third a Rolls-Royce Clyde, both these engines being turbo-props.

The first of the N.11/44 prototypes was taken to the A & AEE Boscombe Down for first flight and this was made by Westland chief test pilot Harold Penrose on December 16 1946. On October 15 1947 this aircraft was lost when propeller bearing failure resulted in a heavy crash landing. The pilot, Squadron Leader Peter Garner, was killed.

From the third prototype, the aircraft were fully equipped for carrier flying and carried the armament fit of four wing-mounted Hispano Mk V cannon. In May 1948, aerodrome dummy deck landings were made at Boscombe Down prior to the carrier trials which were started on June 9 aboard *Implacable*. Further trials were made in *Illustrious* in May and June 1949. The pre-production Wyvern TF Mk 1s (named early in 1947) joined the development programme in 1949 and were used to investigate various aspects of the engine and airframe, including the behaviour of the contra-props, flying controls and armament fits. The fact that the Eagle engine was not comparable with the turbo-prop planned for the production TF Mk 2 meant that nothing could be done to ease the new powerplant into service.

The first of the TF Mk 2 prototypes to fly was the Clyde powered one, making its maiden flight on January 18 1949. This engine was not proceeded with and work was then concentrated on the Python powered version, the first of which flew on March 22 1949. The second Python prototype had a flying life of only two months, being lost on October 31 1949 when Squadron Leader Mike Graves attempted a dead-stick landing after propeller problems. Again the pilot was killed.

In 1948, an order had been placed for 20 pre-production Mark 2s plus a trainer prototype to specification T.12/48. This, the T Mk 3 (Westland W.38), was destined to be a one-off example. Featuring a rearward extension of the cockpit to allow a second seat for the instructor, it flew for the first time on February 11 1950. In November, the machine was destroyed in a crash after engine failure.

The first of the pre-production TF Mk 2s took to the air on February 16 1950 and in June that year made deck landing trials in *Illustrious*, thus becoming the first British seaborne turbo-prop. However, the Python engine was plagued with problems which conspired to delay entry of the Wyvern into squadron service. The definitive production model, firstly designated TF Mk 4 and then S Mk 4 (the S denoting Strike), totalled 94 aircraft of which seven were the last of the pre-production TF Mk 2s built to the Mark 4 standard.

On May 20 1953, the first Wyvern arrived at Ford for No 813 Squadron but even then it and subsequent arrivals were to be used from shore bases only as the engine problems had still not been solved. Not until April 1954 was the fully cleared aircraft available, and, at long last, in September No 813 embarked in *Albion*. A further hiccup occurred with engine flame-outs during catapult launching. On October 13 1954, a remarkable escape was made when Lieutenant B. D. Macfarlane ejected from his Wyvern underwater after ditching

The RAF had also planned to employ it as a fast torpedo fighter replacing the Beaufighter, an early Wyvern TF 1 seen here carrying a torpedo as evidence.

Above left *Naval adaptation meant double wing elements needed to fold on what was a large aeroplane for one engine and one pilot* (Mike Bowyer).

Left *To improve their capability later Wyverns were fitted with Python turbo-prop engines, like WN326, a Mk 4 strike fighter version* (Mike Bowyer).

Above *To compensate for the huge power plant and contra-prop forces meant a taller fin and rudder as finlets on the S Mk 4. In this view one can almost hear the loud whine-cum-scream of the Wyvern!* (Ron Clarke).

from one such abortive catapult launch. In November 1954, No 827 Squadron formed at Ford, the base where the Wyvern training unit, No 703W Flight, also was.

No 813 Squadron returned ashore from *Albion* to re-equip with aircraft modified to solve the flame-out problem and in May 1955 embarked in *Eagle* together with No 827 for a Mediterranean training cruise. Yet again problems were not far away. On May 17, one of 827's Wyverns crashed into *Eagle*'s island in attempting to go round again and left its Python engine embedded in the base of her funnel, necessitating the ship's return to Portsmouth for repairs. On return from the Mediterranean, after completion of the cruise, Nos 813 and 827 Squadrons disembarked to Ford in November and

were disbanded, their aircraft being handed to 830 and 831 Squadrons. In 1956, No 831 joined *Ark Royal* and 830 embarked in *Eagle*. In the autumn, *Eagle* was in the Anglo-French force attacking Suez, Wyverns making their first strikes on November 1. Seventy-nine sorties were mounted in six days and two aircraft were lost, though fortunately their pilots ejected safely.

Nos 830 and 831 disbanded at Ford in January and December 1957 respectively, leaving 813 as the sole front line unit, this having re-formed in October 1956. A final embarkation in *Eagle* began in July 1957 and lasted nine months until the squadron finally disbanded at Ford on March 29 1958. Service in second-line units did not last much longer and the fate of the surviving aircraft was to be sold for scrap to British Aluminium of Warrington.

Westland Wyvern S Mk 4: *Span* 44 ft 0 in (20 ft 0 in folded); *Length* 42 ft 0¼ in; *Height* 15 ft 0 in; *Wing area* 355 sq ft; *Engine* One Armstrong Siddeley Python 3 turbo-prop of 3,670 shp plus 1,180 lb residual jet thrust; *All up weight* 21,200 lb; *Maximum speed* 383 mph at sea level; *Service ceiling* 28,000 ft; *Range* 910 miles (with two 90 gallon drop tanks); *Armament* 4 × 20 mm Hispano cannon and 1 × 2,500 lb torpedo or 3 × 1,000 lb bombs or 16 × 25 lb or 60 lb rocket projectiles.

Hawker Sea Hawk

In May 1946 a contract was issued to Hawker Aircraft for three prototype single-jet aircraft. This followed some two years' work on design studies for possible jet fighters in the hope of obtaining an order for the Royal Air Force. Events were to prove otherwise, as the Air Ministry was of the opinion that the design offered would not be sufficiently superior to the contemporary Gloster Meteor F 4. Of the three prototypes ordered, the first was to be an aerodynamic test airframe and the other two were to be to specification N.7/46 for a naval interceptor. The first aircraft, known as the Hawker P.1040, made its maiden flight from Boscombe Down on September 2 1947 piloted by Bill Humble. A year and a day were to pass before the first of the N.7/46 prototypes took to the air on September 3 1948. This apparently long delay masked the fact that the naval machine was fully equipped for carrier operation from the outset, with folding wings, arrestor hook, catapult spools and the armament installation of four nose-mounted Hispano cannon.

Trials with this aircraft were made on the dummy deck at Boscombe Down before initial carrier tests were started in *Illustrious* in April 1949. These were not altogether successful, as on several occasions the aircraft had to go round again after failing to pick up a wire. As a result, the aircraft was fitted with a lengthened arrestor hook and re-commenced deck trials in October, this time with success. The third of the prototype batch flew on October 17 1949,

already equipped with the longer arrestor hook plus provision to carry underwing drop tanks and RATOG (Rocket Assisted Take-Off Gear). A production contract was awarded that November for 151 Sea Hawks with pressurised cockpit, Martin Baker ejector seat and a 2 ft 6 in increase in span to compensate for weight increase due to added naval equipment.

In 1951, with the Cold War at its height, new military aircraft were accorded 'super priority' status for production with the result that Hawker's capacity was unable to cope with large orders for both the Sea Hawk and the new Hunter. Therefore responsibility for development and production of the naval fighter was transferred to Armstrong Whitworth's Baginton factory after 35 had been built by Hawker at Kingston. Of the Hawker-constructed examples, two were allocated for carrier trials in *Eagle* as part of the type's service evaluation programme. Production proceeded apace through the early 50s with the first Armstrong-Whitworth-built machine making its first flight on December 18

Below *Early Hawker Sea Hawks were fighters, but with some modifications the FB Mk 3 emerged quite early on in the type's programme* (Mike Bowyer).
Right *The Sea Hawk was Hawker's first venture into the jet fighter field, a feature betrayed by the aircraft's straight wing layout. Nevertheless, its close affinity to the Hunter is clearly apparent* (Mike Bowyer).
Below right XE370, *a Sea Hawk FGA 6, leads a Mk 3. Both exhibit the fine, almost delicate, lines of Camm's first venture into jet hardware* (Mike Bowyer).

1952. The initial production versions were the F Mk 1 and F Mk 2, the chief difference of the latter being the introduction of powered aileron controls.

In March 1953, No 806 Squadron became the first front line unit to equip with Sea Hawk F 1s at Brawdy and three months later, on June 15 1953, had the honour of taking part in the fly-past for the Coronation Review of the Fleet at Spithead. On completion of working up, the squadron embarked in *Eagle* on February 2 1954. Two other squadrons received F 1s before the F2 entered service in 1954, joining 802 and 807 Squadrons. No 806 was the first to receive the third variant, the FB Mk 3. This had the ability to carry bombs or mines on the wing pylons with a capacity of up to 1,000 lb each side. The FGA Mk 4 extended the range of weapons further by adding 60 lb rocket projectiles.

Re-engining with uprated Nenes (an extra 200 lb thrust) changed the designations of the FB 3 and FGA 4 to FB Mk 5 and FGA Mk 6. A further batch of Sea Hawks was built new to FGA Mk 6 standard to complete the production of the Royal Navy's Sea Hawks. However, others were built for the Dutch, German and Indian Navies, the latter's continuing to serve until 1982, pending replacement by the Sea Harrier. Six Fleet Air Arm squadrons, in the

Above *Sea Hawk FGA 4,* WV904 *demonstrates the vital arrestor hook. Much experimentation took place with the possibility of jets landing on flexible decks obviating the need for hooks and even undercarriages. Such a system has too many tactical disadvantages* (Mike Bowyer).

Above right *The Sea Hawk 4 was a relatively small aeroplane, wing folding being more straightforward than on many naval aircraft* (Mike Bowyer).

carriers *Albion, Bulwark* and *Eagle,* were involved in the Suez actions in 1956. Their main tasks were the knocking out of military targets, mainly airfields, and giving close support to ground forces. The last carrier-borne squadron to part with its Sea Hawks was *Albion's* No 806 which disbanded at Brawdy on December 15 1960.

Hawker (Armstrong Whitworth) Sea Hawk FGA Mk 6: *Span* 39 ft 0 in (13 ft 4 in folded); *Length* 39 ft 10 in; *Height* 8 ft 9 in; *Wing area* 278 sq ft; *Engine* One 5,200 lb st Rolls-Royce Nene 103; *All up weight* 13,785 lb; *Maximum speed* 560 mph at 36,000 ft; *Service ceiling* 44,500 ft; *Range* 1,400 miles (with two 100 gallon drop tanks); *Armament* 4 × 20 mm Hispano cannon plus 16 × 60 lb rocket projectiles or 4 × 500 lb bombs under wings.

de Havilland Sea Venom

On December 3 1945, Lieutenant Commander E. M. Brown made the world's first deck landing of a jet aircraft when he took the modified Vampire second prototype, *LZ551*, aboard *Ocean*. The Vampire had been semi-navalised by the addition of an arrestor hook, increased flap area and long travel oleo legs and was redesignated Sea Vampire Mk 10. Two days of trials followed the initial landing which led to the placing of an order for further prototypes and a small production batch. Sea Vampires were not assigned to any of the Fleet Air Arm's first-line units but served, in the main, as shore-based trainers, giving jet experience to naval pilots. However, this is not to say that the type saw

The Sea Venom FAW 21 prototype, first flown on March 10 1954 (British Aerospace).

no carrier use at all; much valuable trials work was done to pave the way for the smooth introduction of the fully operational Sea Venom, and six aircraft, modified from Vampire Mk 3 standard to become Sea Vampire F Mk 21s, were used to prove (or disprove) the feasibility of undercarriageless deck-landing. One of the flexible decks built at Farnborough for initial tests was fitted on the flight deck of *Warrior* for seagoing trials in 1949 and the F 21s successfully completed the programme, though in the end the concept was abandoned.

The de Havilland Sea Venom was evolved to meet specification N.107 from the Venom Mk 2 night fighter. The private venture prototype of the night fighter was evaluated by the Royal Navy and there followed a naval prototype Sea Venom NF Mk 20 which began deck trials in *Illustrious* on July 9 1951. The production aircraft, redesignated FAW Mk 20, was equipped with folding wings, a streamlined arrester hook fairing above the jet outlet and a cockpit canopy which could be jettisoned under water if need be. The next variant, the FAW Mk 21, introduced power-operated ailerons, a clear view canopy, ejector seats, a long stroke under-carriage and provision for RATOG. Finally, the substitution of the Ghost 105 engine for the 104 brought about the last mark, the FAW Mk 22.

Delivery to the squadrons commenced with No 890, which received Mk 20s while based ashore at Yeovilton in March 1954. Deck-landing trials with the FAW Mk 21 in *Albion* in the summer of 1954 preceeded the service entry of that model with No 809 Squadron. In the Suez actions of October–November 1956, five Sea Venom squadrons were involved, flying from the aircraft carriers *Albion* and *Eagle*. Their main role was, like the Sea Hawk, to shoot up Egyptian military convoys and airfield installations in support of the ground forces. In the course of this work several MiG-15s were destroyed on the ground. Later work carried out by Sea Venoms included trials with the new de Havilland Firestreak air-to-air guided missiles, No 893 Squadron, embarked in *Victorious*, being responsible for these tests, which were made in the Malta area in December 1958. The targets for the missiles were Fairey Firefly drones and an 80 per cent success rate was claimed. The Firestreak was to form part of the all-missile armament of the Sea Vixen, which began to displace the Sea Venom in 1959 and had completely taken over by the end of 1960.

de Havilland Sea Venom FAW Mk 22: *Span* 42 ft 11 in; *Length* 36 ft 7$\frac{1}{4}$ in; *Height* 8 ft 6$\frac{1}{4}$ in; *Wing area* 279.75 sq ft; *Engine* One 5,300 lb st de Havilland Ghost 105; *All up weight* 15,800 lb; *Maximum speed* 575 mph at sea level; *Service ceiling* 40,000 ft; *Range* 705 miles; *Armament* 4 × 20 mm Hispano cannon plus 8 × 60 lb rocket projectiles or 2 × 500 lb bombs.

Fairey Gannet

The Gannet was the last naval fixed-wing anti-submarine aircraft to enter service before helicopters took over the role. Conceived to meet specification GR.17/45, the aircraft was powered by a double-propeller-turbine, the Armstrong Siddeley Double Mamba, in which one 'half' of the coupled engine could be shut down in the air giving a much extended range. Other benefits that this powerplant offered were a safety margin comparable with a conventional twin-engine layout but with the advantage of an uncluttered folding wing, residual jet thrust from the exhaust outlets and the ability to run on less highly refined fuel eliminated the need for petrol stowage in aircraft carriers. The Gannet also had the combined abilities of hunting and attacking its quarry with a retractable ventral radome for the ASV radar situated aft of a capacious weapon bay, capable of carrying a substantial load. The design was made by a team under the leadership of Fairey's chief designer H. E. Chaplin and chief engineer D. L. Hollis Williams and was known initially as the Type 'Q', then GR.17 after the specification number, before being officially named Gannet.

Three years' work passed between the prototype order, placed by the Ministry of Supply in August 1946, and the appearance of the first prototype in 1949. On September 19 that year, the first aircraft was flown from Aldermaston by chief test pilot Group Captain R. Gordon Slade. Not surprisingly,

it took some time to iron out the bugs before a production order could be placed, nevertheless, the prototype made its first deck landing on *Illustrious* on June 19 1950. Of the three prototypes, the first two were built as two-seaters and the third with three seats, which was to be the arrangement in the production aircraft. The 'super priority' scheme was applied to the Gannet, with the first order being placed in March 1951. Aircraft started to roll off the production line in 1953 and the first of these flew on June 9. October saw the commencement of deck landing trials aboard *Illustrious* and *Eagle*, while other machines carried out manufacturer's tests of engine and radar.

By April 1954, four Gannet AS Mk 1s had been delivered to Ford to join No 703 Squadron's X Flight for service flying trials. On January 17 1955, No 826 Squadron formed on Gannets at Lee-on-Solent and embarked in *Eagle* the following May. With aircraft development and refinement being a continuous process, it was only a matter of months before the succeeding Gannet AS Mk 4 was in the air in prototype form, the first flight occurring on March 12 1956. This version featured an uprated Double Mamba and detail refinements and entered first-line service with No 824 Squadron in August, this unit having been flying AS 1s since February 1955. The 'missing' mark numbers were allocated to the T Mk 2 dual control trainer and the AEW Mk 3 described below. Mention must also be made of the COD Mk 4 which was a carrier-onboard-delivery (communications) aircraft produced by converting AS 4s made redundant by the appearance of Whirlwind anti-submarine helicopters from 1958.

During the mid-50s a requirement was born for

An early production Gannet AS 1, WN360 (Mike Bowyer).

Left *Gannet AS 1* WN353 *in the hands of 700 Squadron, Ford, in 1955.*

Below left *Gannet AS 4* XA412, *the first production Mk 4, first flew on April 13 1956 and is here seen in the hands of 700 Squadron at Ford in 1958* (Mike Bowyer).

Above XA524 *was one of the limited number of Gannet T 2s, identifiable by yellow 'trainer' bands on their aluminium finish. The spiral painted spinner and '320' identify the aircraft as coming from 820 Squadron* (Mike Bowyer).

Above right *A large radome was a prominent feature of the Gannet AEW 3. It operated for many years—but tragically not during the 1982 South Atlantic campaign* (Mike Bowyer).

Right *The Gannet's double engine drove two propellers, the purpose being that one engine/propeller combination could be closed down for economic cruising* (Mike Bowyer).

an airborne early warning aircraft to replace the Douglas Skyraider. To specification AEW.154P Fairey produced the Gannet AEW Mk 3. This entailed an almost complete redesign of the aircraft, the new fuselage featuring the prominent ventral radome taken from the obsolescent Skyraiders and, at first glance, appearing to have but a single cockpit. In fact there was still a crew of three, the two radar observers occupying a cabin within the rear fuselage entered by doors above the trailing edge of the wing. The fin and rudder were of different outline and the jet exhausts discharged below the leading edge of the wing instead of above and behind the wing as in the previous variants. The Mark 3 prototype first flew on August 20 1958 and deck trials were made in *Centaur* in November. Further tests aboard *Victorious* preceeded deliveries to No 700G Squadron for intensive flying trials in 1959. No 700G became A Flight of 849 Squadron on February 1 1960, this being the sole unit to operate the type with its separate flights allocated to carriers as required. C Flight was the first to embark for sea duty in *Hermes* in July 1960. In 1978 the final element of naval AEW was lost when B Flight left

Ark Royal for the last time. This lack of airborne radar cover was to make itself only too apparent in the Falklands conflict of 1982.

Fairey Gannet AS Mk 4: *Span* 54 ft 4 in (19 ft 11 in folded); *Length* 43 ft 0 in; *Height* 13 ft 8½ in; *Wing area* 483 sq ft; *Engine* One 3,035 ehp Armstrong Siddeley Double Mamba 101; *All up weight* 23,446 lb; *Maximum speed* 299 mph; *Service ceiling* 25,000 ft; *Range* 662 miles; *Armament* 2 × homing torpedoes and 3 × depth charges or 2 × mines and 3 × depth charges of 1 × 2,000 lb bomb or 2 × 1,000 lb bombs or 4 × 500 lb bombs; sonobuoys, sea markers and flares—all in the bomb bay: or an underwing load of up to 16 × 60 lb rocket projectiles.

Fairey Gannet AEW Mk 3: *Span* 54 ft 4 in (19 ft 11 in folded); *Length* 44 ft 0 in; *Height* 16 ft 10 in; *Wing area* 483 sq ft; *Engine* One 3,875 ehp Armstrong Siddeley (Rolls-Royce) Double Mamba 102; *All up weight* 25,000 lb; *Maximum speed* 250 mph; *Service ceiling* 25,000 ft; *Range* 700 miles; *Armament* No offensive armament carried.

Supermarine Scimitar

As well as preparing existing aircraft for trials in undercarriageless deck flying, specifications were drawn up for the design of new aircraft which were to be operated from the proposed flexible decks. At the Supermarine division of Vickers, the Type 505 design of 1945 was to lay the foundation of that great company's final indigenous aircraft. Use of a piston engine powerplant would pose problems for an aircraft which was to land on its belly, owing to the need for propeller clearance, so it was almost a foregone conclusion that propulsion would be provided by turbojet. The choice fell upon the Rolls-Royce AJ65 (later Avon) and a pair of these were to be mounted side by side in a broad central fuselage section with flat top and bottom lines providing an excellent base for the revolutionary method of landing. Another unusual feature was that the empennage was to be of butterfly form, mainly to keep these surfaces out of the jet efflux. The whole planes would move in unison for control in pitch with elevators to operate in opposition in

place of the normal rudder for turning.

Before work began on construction, the flexible deck scheme had lost favour and the Type 505 was extensively revised to become a conventional undercarriage design of generally larger dimensions, though of similar layout. The revised aeroplane was called the Type 508 and retained the unswept mainplanes of the original scheme, but a second design was drawn up under the designation of Type 525 to incorporate swept flying surfaces and a conventional fin, following the experience of Swift development from the straight-wing Attacker.

The first of three aircraft to specification N.9/47 flew on August 31 1951 from Boscombe Down with Mike Lithgow at the controls, this being the Type 508. The second prototype, with some refinements, flew as the Type 529 and the more advanced Type 525 took to the air in April 1954. Initial trials in carrier-landing were made by the Type 508 aboard *Eagle* in May 1952. A very important feature of the Type 525 was its boundary layer control flap blowing system. This American-pioneered idea was of great assistance in the low-speed regime in carrier

Below *Last of the Supermarine naval fighters, the Scimitar. XD226 was serving with 700 X Flight when photographed, and later was used by 736 Squadron at Lossiemouth (Mike Bowyer).*

Right *Hook extended, an 807 Squadron Scimitar hurries by (Mike Bowyer).* **Below right** *Scimitar F 1 XD219 was a trials aircraft used both by Supermarine and the A&AEE before it became '617' of 736 Squadron (Mike Bowyer).*

landings. Air bled from the engine compressor was ducted along the trailing edge of the wing and ejected through a narrow slot just upstream of the flap hinge, smoothing the air-flow over the flap and thus providing added lift and lowering the stalling speed.

In 1951 an order for three prototypes to specification N.113D was placed, these being the intermediate stage between the Type 525 and the full production aircraft and known as the Type 544. Mike Lithgow took the first of them for its maiden flight on January 19 1956. Deck-landing trials in *Ark Royal* followed that spring after ADDLs at the RAE Bedford. Though planned as a naval interceptor with an armament of four 30 mm Aden cannon beneath the air intakes, by the mid-50s operational needs had changed the aircraft's role to that of low-level tactical bomber with a nuclear capability. The sturdy airframe of the design stood it in good stead for the rough conditions that would be encountered at these levels. A production order had been placed to specification N.113P in December 1952 for 100 aircraft but of these only 76 were to be built. Service entry of the Scimitar began with intensive trials and training at Boscombe Down and RNAS Ford to familiarise pilots and ground/deck crew with the large and, for that time, advanced machine. No 700X Flight was the Scimitar flying trials unit and the first squadron to form was No 803 at Lossiemouth in June 1958. This unit made the first embarkation of the type in *Victorious* in the following September.

The Scimitar's final first-line role was with No 800 Squadron's B Flight in *Eagle* where their duty was to act as 'buddy pack' refuellers to the Buccaneers of that squadron. The Buccaneer superceded the Scimitar in the tactical strike role as it had the twin advantages of a second crewman and a weapons bay in the fuselage.

Supermarine Scimitar F Mk 1: *Span* 37 ft 2 in (20 ft 6½ in folded); *Length* 55 ft 3 in; *Height* 17 ft 4 in; *Wing area* 484.9 sq ft; *Engines* Two 10,000 lb st Rolls-Royce Avon RA 24 or RA 28 (later Avon 200); *All up weight* 34,200 lb; *Maximum speed* 710 mph at 10,000 ft; *Service ceiling* 46,000 ft; *Range* 1,422 miles; *Armament* 4 × 30 mm Aden cannon and 4 × 1,000 lb bombs or 4 × Bullpup air-to-surface missiles or 4 × 500 lb bombs or 4 × Sidewinder air-to-air missiles or 24 × 3 in rockets (or 4 × 200 gallon drop tanks could be carried on wing pylons).

Westland Whirlwind

In order to secure a good start in helicopter production, Westland Aircraft Limited of Yeovil came to an agreement in 1946 with the American firm Sikorsky for the licence production of their S-51 design. Six US-built S-51s were purchased for initial experience, the first arriving at Yeovil on April 14 1947 and the following year the first Westland-built examples came off the line. One of these, civil registered *G-ALIL*, was delivered to the

Below *The Navy's first large helicopters were Sikorsky S-55 Whirlwinds, two HAS Mk 22s (ex-US Navy H04S-3) of 845 Squadron being seen here* (Mike Bowyer).

Right *Other Whirlwinds were Westland built—and some Westland developed. XM668 was an HAS 7—an anti-submarine aircraft* (Westland Aircraft).

Royal Navy for trials and received the serial *WB810*. Given the name Dragonfly, British production of the machine continued until 1955, many serving with the Navy, mostly in the communications role but also in ship's flights for plane-guard duty.

Following on from their successful initiation with the Dragonfly, Westland proceeded with a similar development of the Sikorsky S-55. One important aspect of this machine was that the engine was mounted in the nose and easily accessible through two large doors. The Royal Navy received a preliminary batch of US-built machines to speed up service introduction under the Mutual Defense Assistance Program. These were of two variants, the HRS-2 transport and the HO4S-3 anti-submarine helicopter, and were given the British designations Whirlwind HAR Mk 21 and HAS Mk 22 respectively.

On October 29 1952, HAR 21s formed the first front line helicopter squadron, No 848, and were quickly into action in Malaya early in the new year, having been transported there in the carrier *Perseus*. They were principally involved in supply dropping and that classic helicopter role, casualty evacuation. The HAS 22s equipped No 706 Squadron for working up and training in the technique of submarine detection with their dunking sonars. The success of the trials led to the formation of 845 Squadron in March 1954 as the first anti-submarine unit, with helicopters handed over from 706, which simultaneously disbanded. So began the Royal Navy's helicopter experience.

The first Westland-built version, the Whirlwind HAR Mk 1, made its first hover on November 12 1952 powered by a 600 hp Pratt & Whitney R-1340-40 and in August 1953 the type's first free flight was achieved. No 705 Squadron used Mark 1s

Whirlwinds have served the British Services well, and in many roles, some most hazardous. XN359 depicted was a Mk 7 used in 1963-1964 by 847 Squadron (Mike Bowyer).

for training. The Whirlwind HAR Mk 2 went into service with the Royal Air Force and the next model to join the Fleet Air Arm was the HAR Mk 3. Power came from a 700 hp Wright R-1300-3 Cyclone. In the Royal Navy this mark served in the communications role and on plane-guard duties with the aircraft carriers. The HAR Mk 5 introduced the British Alvis Leonides Major engine and a drooped tail-cone to give greater rotor clearance in turbulent conditions and led to the HAS Mk 7 which was the first fully effective anti-submarine helicopter. A Mark 3 was modified to serve as a prototype and first flew on October 10 1956. The fuselage was deepened by 6 in and the floor raised to give space for a weapons bay for either a homing torpedo or a dunking sonar, the intention being that the Whirlwinds would operate in pairs, one detecting and the other attacking.

The first production aircraft were delivered to the Navy in the spring of 1957 to No 700H Squadron for intensive flying trials and No 845 Squadron exchanged its old HAS 22s for the new aircraft in August. The next year saw Whirlwinds beginning to replace the Gannet in anti-submarine squadrons with No 820 being the first to do so.

Westland Whirlwind HAS Mk 7: *Rotor diameter* 53 ft 0 in; *Height* 13 ft $2\frac{1}{2}$ in; *Fuselage length* 41 ft $8\frac{1}{2}$ in (rotors turning 62 ft $1\frac{1}{2}$ in); *Engine* One 750 hp Alvis Leonides Major; *All up weight* 7,800 lb; *Maximum speed* 109.5 mph at sea level; *Service ceiling* 9,400 ft; *Range* 334 miles; *Armament* 1 × homing torpedo or anti-submarine bombs or depth charges or anti-submarine sonar dunker.

de Havilland Sea Vixen

To replace the Sea Venom, plans were afoot to produce a modified version under the designation D.H.116. This would feature a new thin section swept back wing mated to a Sea Venom fuselage equipped with the latest radar. However, before metal was cut for this project a change of mind was brought about when the Royal Air Force rejected the D.H.110 in favour of the Gloster Javelin. The twin-engined D.H.110 was seen to offer a better capability than a re-work of the single-engined Venom. Therefore, the second prototype D.H.110 was fitted out for touch-and-go trials aboard *Albion*,

these taking place on September 23 1954. Meanwhile, an interim 'prototype', designated Sea Vixen Mk 20X, had been ordered and was under construction and this made its first flight on June 20 1955. After the usual land-based preliminary trials this aircraft made the first full carrier-arrested landing on *Ark Royal* on April 5 1956. Just under a year later the first production Sea Vixen FAW Mk 1 flew at Christchurch on March 20 1957. The first two aircraft from the production line underwent intensive pre-service trials at A & AEE Boscombe Down and at RAE Bedford and carried out more seagoing tests in the carriers *Ark Royal* and *Centaur*.

November 1957 saw the start of the working up

De Havilland Sea Vixen FAW 1 XJ488 (De Havilland photo).

programme with Y Flight, No 700 Squadron, during which *Victorious* played host for three weeks of deck trials including night landings. Another year and a half passed before the Sea Vixen was declared ready for service and No 892 Squadron formed at Yeovilton on July 2 1959. The unit embarked in *Ark Royal* for its first tour of duty in February 1960.

The Sea Vixen represented a major advance in capability for the Fleet Air Arm. For the first time, shell-firing cannon had been omitted in favour of an all-missile armament, chief amongst which was a fit of four wing-pylon-mounted infra-red homing Fire-streaks. Smaller rockets were also carried and bombs could be fitted for strike missions. The Firestreak, which was an early example of British guided missile technology, had a drawback in that it could only be fired from a position of pursuit in order to be sure of a successful homing. When the Sea Vixen FAW Mk 2 was introduced in 1964, the missile problem was remedied by replacing the early Firestreak with the more sensitive Red Top which could be fired from any interception course.

The FAW Mk 2 had an increased fuel capacity with the addition of extra fuel tanks in forward extensions of the tail booms. Many Mark 1s were converted to the new standard. No 899 Squadron, allocated to *Eagle*, was the first unit to receive the new mark in July 1964. As well as having increased internal fuel capacity, the capability of in-flight refuelling was added by the fitting of Flight Refuelling Limited's Mk 20 drogue refuelling pack, the receiver aircraft taking on fuel by means of a probe fitted outboard of the port tail boom.

The Sea Vixen was destined to be the last British-built conventional naval fighter. Just as the Mark 2 was coming into service, the Royal Navy was thrown into turmoil over the proposed run-down of the aircraft carrier with the contraction of overseas commitments. The Sea Vixens of *Eagle*'s 899 Squadron were present at the withdrawal from Aden in 1967 which was just one example of the retreat. No 899 was also the last squadron to operate Sea Vixens in their true nautical environment until the paying-off of *Eagle* for the last time in 1972. However, old squadrons never die, No 899, equipped with a certain 'bird of prey', was in the forefront of Operation *Corporate*, the repossession of the Falkland Islands in 1982.

de Havilland Sea Vixen FAW Mk 2: *Span* 51 ft 0 in (22 ft 3 in folded), *Length* 55 ft 7 in; *Height* 10 ft 9 in; *Wing area* 648 sq ft; *Engines* Two 11,230 lb st Rolls-Royce Avon 208; *All up weight* 41,575 lb; *Maximum speed* 690 mph at sea level; *Service ceiling* 48,000 ft; *Armament* 28 × 2 in rockets in twin packs in nose and 4 × Red Top a-a missiles or 4 × 500 lb or 2 × 1,000 lb bombs or 4 × rocket pods on wing pylons.

Below *The Sea Vixen began as an all-weather fighter for the RAF. Fighter-bomber variants were later planned, and a specialised trainer variant. For naval purposes additional range was required. Extension of the twin booms gave room for extra fuel as can be seen here. This version was the Mk 2 (Mike Bowyer).*

Right *A Sea Vixen Mk 2 carrying a mixed weapons load including Microcell rocket pods. An IFR probe protrudes from the aircraft, refuelling usually being undertaken from a suitably modified Sea Vixen which carried a special fitment (British Aerospace).*

Westland Wessex

The next step up the ladder of anti-submarine helicopter development came with a further licence agreement with Sikorsky for Westland production of the S-58. A single US Navy HSS-1 airframe was imported to serve as a prototype and this was fitted with a Napier Gazelle gas turbine engine, instead of the American powerplant of a Wright R-1820-84 piston engine. The modified helicopter first flew on May 17 1957 and was followed by the building of two pre-production machines for naval trials, the first of these taking to the air on June 20 1958.

The next year saw full-scale production getting under way of the Westland Wessex HAS Mk 1. The Wessex's chief improvements over the Whirlwind were in its greater speed, range and payload, coupled with auto-stabilisation and a limited night sortie capability. It was, however, still necessary to operate as a two-aircraft team on hunter-killer missions unless they were of short duration, when a

single machine could manage both operations. Whereas the Whirlwind carried its weapons in a bay in the underside, the Wessex slung its torpedoes outside the fuselage, one along each side.

No 700H Squadron was reconstituted in June 1960 at Culdrose to begin intensive flying trials which occupied the next year, the helicopters being handed over to No 815 Squadron at its formation on July 4 1961. In September, 815 embarked in *Ark Royal* for its first carrier deployment and by the end of 1961, Nos 814 and 819 Squadrons had also received the Wessex. Continuous development of sonar, air-to-surface radar and automatic flight control systems led to the appearance of the Wessex HAS Mk 3 which flew in prototype form during 1966. The increase in the amount of electronic equipment which had to be crammed in was responsible for the distinctive dorsal hump in the fairing aft of the rotor head. The air-to-surface search radar was housed in a radome just behind the aforementioned hump. The Wessex's operational

capability in anti-submarine work was now advanced to the state where all phases of flight were fully automated with duplicated systems to cover any failure. All but three of the total of HAS Mk 3s were produced by conversion of Mark 1s.

Yet again, No 700H Squadron re-formed to prepare the Mark 3 for service in January 1967 with 814 Squadron being the first to receive them into the front line in October. In addition to their service in the fleet aircraft carriers, anti-submarine Wessexes were also operated from the County class guided missile destroyers, beginning with *Devonshire* in 1962. These ships' flight Wessexes were parented initially by 829 Squadron and latterly by 737

The Westland Wessex HAS 1 entered Royal Navy service in 1960 and gradually replaced the Whirlwind.

Squadron (from 1970 when the former unit specialised on the Wasp).

Westland Wessex HAS Mk 3: *Rotor diameter* 56 ft 0 in; *Height* 14 ft 5 in; *Fuselage length* 48 ft 4½ in (rotors turning 65 ft 10½ in); *Engine* One 1,600 shp Napier Gazelle 165; *All up weight* 13,500 lb; *Maximum speed* 127 mph at sea level; *Service ceiling* 14,100 ft; *Range* 390 miles; Armament 2 × homing torpedoes or anti-submarine sonar dunker.

Blackburn Buccaneer

The Royal Navy's most powerful and advanced British-built aircraft, the Blackburn B.103 Buccaneer, was conceived in 1952 in response to the Admiralty's Naval Aircraft requirement NA39. This called for a high performance carrier-borne strike aircraft able to attack targets at very low level with an internally stowed weapon load, including if necessary a nuclear store. The requirement had been drawn up as a counter to the Soviet Sverdlov class cruisers after consideration had at first been given to the development of a new surface vessel. A powerful carrier-borne attack aircraft was seen to offer a very flexible weapon which would not be tied to the maritime attack role, should other tasks arise.

Many of the major British airframe manufacturers produced designs to the official specification, M.148T, which gave detail to the basic NA39 requirement. Blackburn's design was selected in

July 1955 after almost three years of work and an initial order was placed for a development batch of 20 aircraft. One of the major essentials was a radius of action of 400 nautical miles carrying a full weapon load. This to be combined with a take-off performance compatible with flight deck operation. To provide sufficient lift while keeping the wing small enough to fold for carrier stowage, the American-pioneered boundary layer blowing system was incorporated. A pair of de-rated de Havilland Gyron Junior engines was selected for the powerplant to keep fuel consumption down and the fuselage was carefully area-ruled for optimum high subsonic speed performance, this producing the distinctive swelling in line with the wing trailing edge.

It took another three years to build the aircraft, part of this time being taken up by the design of a milling machine to produce the wing skin panels from single slabs of alloy. Nevertheless, the target of

Westland Wessex HAS 1, XP118, of 737 Squadron, Portland (Mike Bowyer).

Above *The Blackburn NA39 Buccaneer 1, XK489, the fourth prototype, first flew on January 31 1959 and was used for carrier trials* (Mike Bowyer).

Below XK534, *a production Buccaneer S 1 used for trials by 700Z Flight in 1961, prior to service with 809 Squadron* (Mike Bowyer).

A low pass by a Buccaneer S 1, XN928, *of 801 Squadron* (Mike Bowyer).

first flight in April 1958 was met. Constructed in the Brough factory, the first aircraft, *XK486*, was moved by road to RAE Bedford, whence it flew on the last day of the projected month with Lieutenant-Commander Derek Whitehead as pilot and Bernard Watson as flight test observer. There followed an intensive programme of trials with the development aircraft, leading up to the first deck-landing on *Victorious* in January 1960.

The first service unit to form was No 700Z Squadron, the flying trials unit based at Lossiemouth, and this was followed by the first operational squadron, No 801. This embarked in *Ark Royal* in February 1963, all the Buccaneers being painted in the anti-nuclear flash white with 60 per cent reflectivity markings as were the RAF's V-Bombers. No 809 Squadron formed at Lossiemouth, as a shore-based unit to begin with, and in 1964 the second seagoing squadron, No 800, embarked in *Eagle.* This completed the service allocation of the Gyron-powered Buccaneer S Mk 1.

Meanwhile, work had been progressing on the next mark, the S Mk 2, which had a significant increase in radius of action by the substitution of a new engine. The Rolls-Royce RB.168 had been developed as an economic turbofan for a civil airliner, the de Havilland Trident. When installed in the Buccaneer it increased thrust by about a third over the Gyron, while its lower fuel consumption gave the increased endurance. Two of the development aircraft were re-engined with the Spey to serve as S Mk 2 prototypes and in this form first

flew on May 17 1963. In June 1964 the first production Buccaneer S 2 flew and aircraft soon began to equip No 700B Squadron for service trials. All three front line S 1 squadrons re-equipped with S 2s between 1965 and 1967 and in the latter year No 803 also formed on the type.

Thankfully, the Buccaneer was never required to fly in anger but very useful deterrence flights were made around Singapore at the time of the Indonesian confrontation, in the controversial withdrawal from Aden in 1968 and in Belize. Nearer to home, the type showed its capabilities in the 'attacks' on the supertanker *Torrey Canyon* wrecked on the Seven Stones reef off the Scilly Isles in March 1967. From the mid-60s the government decided to phase out the aircraft carrier, and, with it, the fixed wing element of the Fleet Air Arm. This was to be complete by the mid-70s but a reprieve was given to extend the life of *Ark Royal* which had been extensively refitted to operate Phantoms. In December 1978, the *Ark Royal* was paid off for the last time and her Buccaneers, No 809 Squadron, went the way of their erstwhile companions—to the shore-based squadrons of the Royal Air Force.

Blackburn (Hawker Siddeley) Buccaneer S Mk 2: *Span* 44 ft 0 in (19 ft 11 in folded); *Length* 63 ft 5 in; *Height* 16 ft 3 in; *Wing area* 514.7 sq ft; *Engines* Two 11,100 lb st Rolls-Royce Spey 101; *All up weight* 62,000 lb; *Maximum speed* 645 mph at 250 ft; *Range* 2,300 miles; *Armament* 4,000 lb of bombs in fuselage plus 4 × wing pylons for bombs or Martel air-to-surface missiles.

McDonnell Phantom

Entry of the Phantom into the Royal Navy was a direct result of the political upheavals of the mid-60s in connection with the British aircraft industry. As a Sea Vixen replacement, attention had been focused on the advanced V/STOL aircraft developed from the Hawker P.1127 (Harrier forerunner) known as the P.1154. Two versions were to be built, one each for the Royal Navy and Royal Air Force. However, in 1964, the naval aircraft was cancelled. (The RAF version went too, in 1965.) As no other suitable new aircraft was under development in Britain, it was necessary to look to America for an alternative. The type chosen for both services was the McDonnell Phantom, the F-4J variant of which was then under development for the US Navy and Marine Corps.

In order to soften the blow to the British industry it was intended that 50 per cent of the programme cost would be spent at home. The General Electric J79 engine was to be replaced by a new model of the Rolls-Royce Spey and this alone would require re-engineering of the fuselage to accept the larger powerplant. The former Blackburn factory at Brough, which was then part of the Hawker Siddeley group which had been deprived of the P.1154, was

Symbolically, Phantom 1, XT872, of 892 Squadron carries an omega device on the fin (Mike Bowyer).

given the job of working with McDonnell on the modifications. Of the many alterations necessary, some of the most important were those to enable the aircraft to operate from the RN carriers which were smaller than their American counterparts. The arrestor hook and main gear legs were strengthened to allow for a heavier landing, the forward under-carriage leg was made to extend 40 in to increase the angle of attack for catapult launching and a slotted tailplane, drooped ailerons and larger flaps were added to augment lift on take-off.

The RN Phantom was given the US designation F-4K and the first prototype YF-4K flew at St Louis on June 27 1966. The first production aircraft flew on November 2 1966 but deliveries did not begin until 1968. Three aircraft were delivered to No 700P Squadron, the intensive flying trials unit, at Yeovilton on April 25 1968. When the Phantom had been ordered, 52 (including four prototypes) of the naval version, to be designated FG Mk 1, had been included but by the time deliveries commenced the

McDonnell F-4K Phantom 1 of 767 Squadron touches down at Yeovilton (Mike Bowyer).

fixed wing element of the Fleet Air Arm was being cut back, so that 20 of the batch were transferred directly to the Royal Air Force. On January 14 1969, No 767 Squadron was formed for flying training and on March 31 the sole first-line unit, No 892 Squadron, formed, their fin insignia incorporating the Greek letter omega as a reference to their status as the Navy's last fixed-wing carrier-borne squadron.

Deck-landing trials were carried out in *Eagle* in June 1969 but that ship was not fully equipped to operate Phantoms and was to be withdrawn from service in 1972. *Ark Royal*, which was to be 892's seagoing home, was under refit, so a deployment was made to the USS *Saratoga* in the Mediterranean to gain operational experience. Four Phantoms were detached for this operation after carrying out catapult launch trials from the dummy deck at RAE Bedford, the first one landing-on on October 9 1969. Owing to the steep inclination of the British Phantom from the 40 in extensible nosewheel leg,

the jet efflux in reheat burnt out a section of *Saratoga*'s deck—which must have caused a few red faces. The trials were otherwise fully successful and six 892 crews carrier qualified. They were presented with a section of the scorched deck to keep as a souvenir of the occasion!

In April 1970, trials began in *Ark Royal* and on June 12 the full squadron strength of 12 aircraft joined the ship for working up. The first operational deployment began on September 4 1970 and for the next eight years the Phantoms formed part of the ship's complement. During this period they gained a wide audience on television in the BBC series 'Sailor', recorded in 1976. When *Ark Royal* paid off for the last time at the end of 1978 her Phantoms were handed over to the Royal Air Force.

McDonnell Phantom FG Mk 1: *Span* 38 ft 5 in; *Length* 58 ft 3 in; *Height* 16 ft 3 in; *Wing area* 538 sq ft; *Engines* Two 12,250 lb st (20,515 reheat) Rolls-Royce Spey 202/203; *All up weight* 54,600 lb; *Maximum speed* Mach 2.5 in reheat (about 1,500 mph); *Service ceiling* 70,000 ft; *Combat radius* 967 miles; *Armament* 4 × Sparrow (under fuselage) and 4 × Sidewinder (under wings) air-to-air guided missiles or 10,000 lb of conventional or nuclear bombs.

Westland Sea King

Sea King HAS 1 XV370 *'dunking' its sonar* (Westland Aircraft).

When a replacement was sought for the Wessex anti-submarine helicopter, it was hoped that an indigenous design could be drawn up to fit the bill. This was to be the Westland WG.1 project which stemmed from the tandem rotor Bristol Types 173 and 192. Sad to say, it was not to be, for confusion ensued when an attempt was made to combine the naval need with a Royal Air Force/Army requirement for a heavy lift helicopter. The only way out of the impasse was to turn again to America. The object of attention was the Sikorsky S-61, in particular the SH-3D model. Unlike the Whirlwind and Wessex, which were extensively re-engineered for British production, the Sea King was to receive a minimum of alteration in order to get the aircraft into service more quickly.

Four American-built helicopters were ordered, one delivered by ship already assembled and three sets of components for erection in England. The ready-made machine served as the prototype and first flew in Britain on October 10 1966. The three Sea Kings assembled by Westland at Yeovil were fitted with British-built engines, General Electric T58s licence-built by Rolls-Royce as the Gnome H.1400, and the first of these flew on September 8 1967. They were used to make the development trials while production got under way of the HAS Mk 1. Fifty-six aircraft were built under the first production order and the first Westland Sea King HAS Mk 1 took to the air on May 7 1969. No time

was wasted in delivering the aircraft to the Royal Navy, with No 700S Squadron being formed at Culdrose in August for intensive flying trials, the first helicopter being delivered on August 11. The crew training programme got under way with formation of No 706 Squadron, also at Culdrose, in November 1969 to be soon followed by 737 Squadron at Portland, whence the fully trained crews would proceed to first-line squadrons.

The Sea King's armament consists of homing torpedoes or depth charges plus the essential dunking sonar to detect the submarine under water. A further piece of equipment, not in fact fitted in the American SH-3D, is the air and surface search radar mounted beneath the prominent dorsal radome. No 824 Squadron formed on the Sea King to serve in *Ark Royal* in February 1970 to be followed in April by No 826 for *Eagle*. Introduction of an uprated engine, improved transmission and six-bladed tail rotor brought about redesignation to HAS Mk 2, 21 aircraft being new-built and conversion sets being supplied for the updating of Mark 1s. Run down of the RN carrier force resulted in a steady reshuffle of squadrons, progressing from ship to ship amongst the commando carriers *Bulwark* and *Hermes*, the anti-submarine cruisers *Tiger* and *Blake* and several Royal Fleet Auxiliaries. More recently 826 has been allocated to *Hermes*, since she was converted to operate Sea Harriers, and 820 Squadron to *Invincible*, both these units putting in many hours of flying time in the Falklands crisis in the spring of 1982.

From January 1979, development proceeded on the HAS Mk 5, one Mark 2 being converted to serve as prototype and 17 new aircraft being built. The most important new feature of this variant is the Sea Searcher radar mounted in the dorsal position beneath a larger radome and doubling the range of the earlier equipment. First flight was made on August 1 1980 and deliveries began on October 2, the receiver squadron being *Invincible*'s No 820. Fifty-two HAS 2s are being modified to the new standard. The disabling by Exocet missile of the destroyer *Sheffield* on May 4 1982 reinforced the need to provide an airborne early warning aircraft to fill the gap left by the disappearance from the Navy of the Fairey Gannet. Eight and a half weeks of intensive work by an MoD/manufacturer team produced the first Westland Sea King HAS Mk 2A, fitted with the powerful Thorn-EMI Searchwater radar. This equipment is carried in a large radome

just aft of the sliding door on the starboard side of the fuselage, in such a way that it swings down from stowed position through 90 degrees to give a 360 degree scan below the helicopter. Two machines thus modified were allocated to D Flight of 824 Squadron for embarkation in *Illustrious*, which sailed for the South Atlantic on August 2 1982 to relieve *Invincible*.

For the future, work is proceeding as a joint venture between Westland and the Italian firm Augusta on a multi-role helicopter, one variant of which is planned to begin replacing the Sea King in 1990. As yet no name has been assigned to the machine which bears the designation EH-101. This is the first project to be developed by EH Industries Ltd, the Anglo-Italian subsidiary company, set up in June 1980. The powerplant is at present planned to be three General Electric T700 turboshafts powering a single main gearbox, and a triple hydraulic system will impart a high degree of failure survivability. Current timing allows for first flight of a pre-production machine in 1986.

Westland Sea King HAS Mk 5: *Rotor diameter* 62 ft 0 in; *Height* 15 ft 6 in; *Fuselage length* 55 ft 9¾ in (rotors turning 72 ft 8 in); *Engines* Two 1,660 shp Rolls-Royce Gnome H.1400-1; *All up weight* 16,341 lb; *Maximum speed* 129 mph at sea level; *Range* 764 miles; *Armament* 4 × homing torpedoes Mks 44, 46 or Stingray or 4 × depth charges Mk 11.

Sea King XV648 of 826 Squadron, then operated from HMS Blake, running up on the Fleet during the 1977 Jubilee Naval Review (Mike Bowyer).

British Aerospace Sea Harrier

Although the Fleet Air Arm was to have been equipped with a V/STOL aeroplane in the mid-60s in the shape of the P.1154, this was cancelled along with the RAF version and conventional high performance aircraft, Phantoms, purchased instead. In February 1963, Hawker test pilot Bill Bedford had taken the P.1127 prototype *XP831* aboard *Ark Royal*. Numerous trials with Harriers were made in many ships of several navies, ranging from fleet carriers such as *Eagle* to auxiliaries with nothing larger than a helicopter platform. The US Marine Corps regularly operated their AV-8As from their so-called sea control ships and Spain acquired Harriers via the USA specifically to be flown from their aged wooden-decked aircraft carrier *Dédalo*.

Design staff at Kingston had not neglected the study of dedicated maritime V/STOL since P.1154 was axed but no government money was forthcoming for detailed development and production. However, as late as 1972, things began to happen. The naval architects had drawn up the design for what was usually referred to as an anti-submarine cruiser, which in fact was a small aircraft carrier

fitted to carry, and operate with, a team of anti-submarine helicopters. While all this was going on, defence expenditure was being steadily eroded, in standard peacetime fashion, and the RN fleet carrier force had dropped to one, when realisation dawned that there would be no flexible air defence for the fleet at sea. The policy had been that the RAF would look after the air protection of naval forces while the Navy itself was devoted to specialised anti-submarine warfare, all this confined to North Atlantic waters on assignment to NATO. Fortunately greater sense prevailed and a Maritime

Harrier was drawn up to operate from the new vessels. It was thought that an order would be placed for about two dozen aircraft in 1973 but this plan was scotched by the onset of inflation, union and energy crises, multiple general elections and further Defence Reviews. So it was not until May 1975 that the Defence Minister, Mr Roy Mason, at last announced the go-ahead for a batch of 24 Sea Harriers (plus one trainer) and two more carriers.

The design that was selected was for a 'minimum cost, minimum risk' conversion of the standard Harrier, in which the most noticeable difference would be the new forward fuselage. This would introduce a nose radome to house the Ferranti Blue Fox radar for air-to-air and air-to-surface search and a completely revised cockpit layout, raised 11 in to give much improved view and making room available underneath for further electronic equipment, notably the Doppler radar nav-aid. The new radome was designed to hinge to port to give ready access to the equipment within. To reduce susceptibility to corrosion in the marine atmosphere, several components would be made from more resistant materials, for example, the Harrier's magnesium engine fan casting would be replaced by one of forged aluminium.

Once the order had been placed, construction proceeded steadily and was rewarded with a first flight on August 20 1978 by John Farley at Dunsfold. In November the first deck-landing was made on *Hermes* by Sea Harrier *XZ450* for trials together with single- and two-seat Harriers. On June 18 1979, the first delivery was made to Yeovilton, where the IFTU No 700A Squadron had formed in May, this unit subsequently becoming 899 Squadron. On April 23 1980, No 800 Squadron was formed and allocated to *Invincible*, the first of the new light carriers.

Less than two years later, the Sea Harrier was to be proved in no uncertain terms. The Argentine invasion of the Falkland Islands on April 2 1982 brought an immediate response from the government in Britain in the rapid despatch of a powerful Naval Task Force. The Sea Harriers were a vital element of this, almost all available machines being despatched to the South Atlantic in *Invincible* and *Hermes*, the latter acting as flagship of Rear-Admiral John Woodward. If convincing proof were needed of

Background photograph *Sea Harriers of 809 NAS* en route *to the South Atlantic* (British Aerospace).

Sea Harrier armed with Sidewinders (MoD).

the efficacy of the Sea Harrier this operation was to provide it, for although seven aircraft were to be lost through accident or ground-based anti-aircraft artillery fire, none was to succumb in air-to-air combat, chiefly with Mirages. At least 20 Argentine aircraft were destroyed, either by Sidewinder missiles or 30 mm cannon fire, others perhaps being lost on the long return flight to the mainland. The story of the Falklands conflict has been widely told although it will probably be many years before full details of some aspects are known. However, one thing that it made abundantly clear to those who did not know or who had again forgotten was the invaluable contribution that ship-based fixed wing aircraft make to air protection of the fleet and

ground forces striving to secure a bridgehead. The action was also instrumental in the reversal of the plan to sell *Invincible* to Australia at a bargain price.

British Aerospace Sea Harrier FRS Mk 1: *Span* 25 ft 3 in; *Length* 47 ft 7 in; *Height* 11 ft 10 in; *Wing area* 201.1 sq ft; *Engine* One 21,500 lb st Rolls-Royce Pegasus 104; *All up weight* 26,000 lb; *Maximum speed* 740 mph at sea level; *Service ceiling* 51,200 ft; *Tactical radius* 500 miles; *Armament* 2 × 30 mm Aden cannon in under-fuselage pods and 2 × Sidewinder air-to-air guided missiles on wing pylons or up to 5,000 lb of bombs.

Appendix

A summary of the main aircraft carrier allocations of flights and squadrons

The purpose of the following list is to provide a guide to the operation of carrier-borne aircraft in Royal Navy service with particular regard to the expansion and contraction of the Fleet Air Arm throughout its existence. During the Second World War in particular, squadrons often moved from ship to ship as circumstances demanded and to attempt a complete listing would distort the overall scale. Further detail on the subject may be gleaned from volumes listed in the bibliography below. Observant readers will quickly notice some question marks in the dates given. If anyone can fill any of these gaps the author would be pleased to hear from them, care of the publisher.

Up to about 1920, ship-borne aeroplanes were generally allocated to their parent ships, or, as in the case of the Tondern raid, taken aboard as needed. By that token, types covered in the early part of this book served in the following ships:

Sopwith Pup	*Vindex, Manxman, Vindictive, Furious, Argus*
Beardmore WB III	*Nairana, Pegasus, Furious*
Sopwith 1½-strutter	*Vindex, Furious, Argus*
Sopwith 2F 1 Camel	*Pegasus, Furious, Argus, Eagle*
Grain Griffin	*Vindictive*
Sopwith Cuckoo	*Furious, Eagle, Argus* (185 Sqn, 1918)
Parnall Panther	205 Sqn *Argus* 1919–21
	441 Flt *Hermes* 1924
Nieuport Nightjar	401 Flt *Argus* 1923–24
Supermarine Seagull II	440 Flt *Eagle* 1924
Blackburn Dart	460 Flt *Eagle* 1924–30
	461 Flt *Furious* 1924–30
	462 Flt *Furious* 1925–29
	463 Flt *Courageous* 1928–33
	464 Flt *Courageous* 1928–33

Avro Bison	421A Flt *Furious* 1925–??
	421B Flt *Eagle* 1927
	423 Flt *Argus* 1924–25, *Hermes* 1926, *Eagle* 1926–29
Blackburn Blackburn	420 Flt *Furious* 1925–29
	422 Flt *Argus* 1923, 1928–29, *Eagle* 1924
	449 Flt *Furious* 1929–30, *Courageous* 1930–31
	450 Flt *Argus* 1929–31
Fairey IIID	440 Flt *Eagle* 1925, *Hermes* 1926
	441 Flt *Hermes* 1924–26, *Eagle* 1926, *Argus* 1926–29
	442 Flt *Argus* 1925–29, *Hermes* 1930
	443A Flt *Furious* 1925–26
	443B Flt *Argus* 1927–28
	443 Composite Flt *Furious* 1927
	445 Flt *Courageous* 1929
Fairey Flycatcher	401 Flt *Argus* 1924–25, 1928–29, *Eagle* to *Hermes* 1926, *Courageous* 1930–31, *Furious* 1932–33
	402 Flt *Eagle* 1924–30, *Courageous* 1932
	403 Flt *Hermes* 1924–32
	404B Flt *Argus* 1927
	404 Flt *Courageous* 1928, *Argus* 1929–??
	405 Flt *Furious* 1926–30, *Glorious* 1930–32
	406 Flt *Glorious* 1930–32
	407 Flt *Courageous* 1928–30, *Furious* 1931–32
	408 Flt *Glorious* 1930
	801 Sqn *Furious* 1933
Fairey IIIF	421 Flt *Furious* 1928–29
	440 Flt *Hermes* 1927–33
	441 Flt *Argus* 1930, *Glorious* 1930–33
	442 Flt *Furious* 1932–33
	443 Composite Flt *Furious* 1927
	443 Flt *Furious* 1928–29
	445 Flt *Courageous* 1928–33
	446 Flt *Courageous* 1928–33
	447 Flt *Furious* 1929, *Glorious* 1930–32
	448 Flt *Eagle* 1929–30, *Glorious* 1931–33

449 Flt *Courageous* 1931, *Furious* 1932–33
450 Flt *Courageous* 1930–33
460 Flt *Glorious* 1932–33, *Eagle* 1933
820 Sqn *Courageous* 1933
822 Sqn *Furious* 1933–36
823 Sqn *Glorious* 1933–35
824 Sqn *Eagle* 1933–34
825 Sqn *Glorious* 1933–36

Blackburn Ripon
460 Flt *Eagle* 1930, *Glorious* 1931–32
461 Flt *Glorious* 1930–33
462 Flt *Furious* 1929, *Glorious* 1930–33
465 Flt *Furious* 1931–33
466 Flt *Furious* 1931–33
811 Sqn *Furious* 1933–36

Blackburn Baffin
810 Sqn *Courageous* 1933–36
811 Sqn *Furious* 1936
812 Sqn *Glorious* 1934–36

Hawker Osprey
404 Flt *Courageous* 1932–33
409 Flt *Glorious* 1932–33
800 Sqn *Courageous* 1933–??, *Ark Royal* 1938
801 Sqn *Furious* 1933–??
802 Sqn *Glorious* 1933–??
803 Sqn *Eagle* 1933–34, *Hermes* 1935–??, *Ark Royal* 1938

Hawker Nimrod
401 Flt *Furious* 1932–33
402 Flt *Courageous* 1932–33
404 Flt *Courageous* 1932–33
408 Flt *Glorious* 1932–33
409 Flt *Glorious* 1932–33
800 Sqn *Courageous* 1933–37
801 Sqn *Furious* 1933–38
802 Sqn *Glorious* 1933–39
803 Sqn *Eagle* 1933–34, *Hermes* 1935–??

Fairey Seal
820 Sqn *Courageous* 1933–35
821 Sqn *Courageous* 1933–36
822 Sqn *Furious* 1936–38
823 Sqn *Glorious* 1935–36
824 Sqn *Hermes* 1934–??, *Eagle* 19??–38

Blackburn Shark
810 Sqn *Courageous* 1936–38
820 Sqn *Courageous* 1935–38
821 Sqn *Courageous* 1936–??, *Furious* 19??

Fairey Swordfish
807 Sqn *Hunter* 1944
810 Sqn *Ark Royal* 1938–41, *Illustrious* 1942
811 Sqn *Furious* 1936–39, *Courageous* 1939, *Biter* 1943, *Vindex* 1944
812 Sqn *Glorious* 1936–40, *Argus* 1941, *Furious* 1941, *Ark Royal* 1941
813 Sqn *Eagle* 1937–42, *Illustrious* 1940, *Campania* 1944–45
814 Sqn *Ark Royal* 1938–39, *Hermes* 1939–41
815 Sqn *Illustrious* 1940
816 Sqn *Furious* 1939–41, *Ark Royal* 1941, *Dasher* 1943, *Tracker* 1943,

Chaser 1944
818 Sqn *Furious* 1939–40, *Ark Royal* 1940–41, *Unicorn* 1943
819 Sqn *Illustrious* 1940, *Archer* 1943, *Activity* 1944
820 Sqn *Ark Royal* 1938–41, *Formidable* 1942
821 Sqn *Ark Royal* 1938–40
821X Flt *Argus* 1940–41
822 Sqn *Courageous* 1938–39
823 Sqn *Glorious* 1936–40
824 Sqn *Eagle* 1938–42, *Illustrious* 1940, *Argus* 1942, *Unicorn* 1943, *Striker* 1943–44
825 Sqn *Glorious* 1936–40, *Furious* 1940–41, 1943, *Argus* 1940- 41, *Victorious* 1941
825 Flt *Avenger* 1941–42
825 Sqn *Ark Royal* 1941, *Vindex* 1944–45
829 Sqn *Formidable* 1941, *Illustrious* 1942
833A Flt *Biter* 1942
833B Flt *Avenger* 1942
833 Sqn *Stalker* 1943–44, *Activity* 1944
834 Sqn *Archer* 1942, *Hunter* 1943, 1944, *Battler* 1943–44
835 Sqn *Battler* 1943, *Nairana* 1944–45
836 Sqn *MAC-Ships* 1943–44
837 Sqn *Dasher* 1943
840 Sqn *MAC-Ships* 1943–44
842 Sqn *Fencer* 1943–44
842 Flt *Furious* 1944
860 Sqn Royal Netherlands Navy MAC-Ships 1943–44

Blackburn Skua
800 Sqn *Ark Royal* 1938–41
801 Sqn *Furious* 1939, 1940–41, *Ark Royal* 1940
803 Sqn *Ark Royal* 1939, 1940, *Glorious* 1940
813 Sqn *Eagle* 1941

Gloster Sea Gladiator
801 Sqn *Courageous* 1939
802 Sqn *Glorious* 1939–40
804 Sqn *Glorious* 1940, *Furious* 1940
813 Sqn *Eagle* 1940, *Illustrious* 1940

Fairey Fulmar
800Z Sqn *Victorious* 1941
800Y Sqn *Argus* 1941
800 Sqn *Furious* 1941, *Indomitable* 1942
803 Sqn *Formidable* 1941
806 Sqn *Illustrious* 1940, 1942, *Formidable* 1941, *Indomitable* 1942
807 Sqn *Furious* 1941, *Ark Royal* 1941, *Argus* 1941–42
808 Sqn *Ark Royal* 1940–41
809 Sqn *Victorious* 1941–42
813 Sqn *Eagle* 1941. *Campania* 1944
882 Sqn *Illustrious* 1942, *Furious* 1942
844 Sqn *Victorious* 1942

Fairey Albacore	817 Sqn *Furious* 1941, *Victorious* 1941–42, *Indomitable* 1943
	820 Sqn *Victorious* 1941–42, *Formidable* 1942–43
	822 Sqn *Furious* 1942–43
	826 Sqn *Formidable* 1941
	827 Sqn *Victorious* 1941, *Indomitable* 1942
	828 Sqn *Victorious* 1941
	829 Sqn *Formidable* 1941
	831 Sqn *Indomitable* 1942
	832 Sqn *Victorious* 1941–42
	882 Sqn *Furious* 1942
Hawker Sea Hurricane	800 Sqn *Indomitable* 1942, *Biter* 1942
	801 Sqn *Eagle* 1942
	802 Sqn *Avenger* 1941–42
	804 Sqn *Dasher* 1942
	807 Sqn *Argus* 1941
	813 Sqn *Eagle* 1942
	824 Sqn *Striker* 1943–44
	825 Sqn *Furious* 1943, *Vindex* 1944
	835 Sqn *Nairana* 1944
	880A Flt *Furious* 1941
	880 Sqn *Indomitable* 1942
	883 Sqn *Avenger* 1941–42
	885 Sqn *Victorious* 1942
	891 Sqn *Dasher* 1942–43
Grumman Wildcat	802B Sqn *Argus* 1941, *Victorious* 1941
	802 Sqn *Audacity* 1941
	806 Sqn *Indomitable* 1942
	809 Sqn *Illustrious* 1943
	811 Sqn *Biter* 1943, *Vindex* 1944
	813 Sqn *Campania* 1944–45
	816 Sqn *Chaser* 1944
	819 Sqn *Activity* 1944
	821 Sqn *Puncher* 1945
	824 Sqn *Striker* 1943–44
	825 Sqn *Vindex* 1945
	832 Sqn *Begum* 1944
	833 Sqn *Activity* 1944
	834 Sqn *Battler* 1944
	835 Sqn *Nairana* 1944–45
	842 Sqn *Fencer* 1943–44, *Campania* 1944–45
	845 Sqn *Ameer* 1944
	846 Sqn *Tracker* 1944, *Trumpeter* 1944–45
	851 Sqn *Shah* 1944
	852 Sqn *Nabob* 1944, *Fencer* 1944
	853 Sqn *Tracker* 1944, *Queen* 1945
	856 Sqn *Premier* 1945
	878 Sqn *Illustrious* 1943
	881 Sqn *Illustrious* 1942, *Furious* 1943, *Pursuer* 1944, *Fencer* 1944, *Trumpeter* 1944, *Premier* 1945
	882 Sqn *Illustrious* 1942, *Victorious* 1942, 1943, *Searcher* 1944–45
	888 Sqn *Formidable* 1942–43, *Unicorn* 1943
	890 Sqn *Illustrious* 1943, *Atheling* 1944
	892 Sqn *Archer* 1943
	893 Sqn *Formidable* 1942–43, *Unicorn* 1943
	896 Sqn *Victorious* 1943, *Pursuer* 1944
	898 Sqn *Victorious* 1943, *Searcher* 1944, *Striker* 1944
Supermarine Seafire (Second World War)	801 Sqn *Furious* 1942–44, *Implacable* 1944–46
	807 Sqn *Furious* 1942, *Indomitable* 1943, *Battler* 1943, *Hunter* 1944–45
	808A Sqn *Battler* 1943
	808 Sqn *Battler* 1943
	809 Sqn *Unicorn* 1943, *Stalker* 1944–45, *Shah* 1945 as spare deck
	816 Sqn *Tracker* 1943
	833 Flt *Stalker* 1943
	834 Flt *Hunter* 1943
	834 Sqn *Battler* 1943–44
	842 Sqn *Fencer* 1943–44
	879 Sqn *Attacker* 1943–44
	880 Sqn *Argus* 1942, *Indomitable* 1943, *Stalker* 1943, *Furious* 1944, *Implacable* 1944–45
	884 Sqn *Victorious* 1942
	885 Sqn *Formidable* 1942–43, *Unicorn* 1943
	886 Sqn *Attacker* 1943, 1944
	887 Sqn *Unicorn* 1943, *Indefatigable* 1944, 1945, *Implacable* 1944
	889 Sqn *Atheling* 1944
	894 Sqn *Illustrious* 1943, *Unicorn* 1943, *Indefatigable* 1944, 1945, *Implacable* 1944
	897 Sqn *Unicorn* 1943
	899 Sqn *Indomitable* 1943, *Hunter* 1943, *Khedive* 1944
Supermarine Seafire (post-war)	800 Sqn *Triumph* 1947–50
	802 Sqn *Vengeance* 1946, *Venerable* 1946
	804 Sqn *Theseus* 1947, *Ocean* 1948, 1949
	805 Sqn *Ocean* 1946
	806 Sqn *Glory* 1946–47
	807 Sqn *Implacable* 1947, *Vengeance* 1947
Fairey Barracuda	810 Sqn *Illustrious* 1943–44
	812 Sqn *Vengeance* 1945–46
	814 Sqn *Venerable* 1945–46
	815 Sqn *Indomitable* 1944
	817 Sqn *Indomitable* 1944
	820 Sqn *Indefatigable* 1944
	821 Sqn *Puncher* 1945
	822 Sqn *Victorious* 1944
	826 Sqn *Indefatigable* 1944, *Formidable* 1944
	827 Sqn *Furious* 1943, 1944, *Victorious* 1944, *Formidable* 1944, *Colossus* 1945

	828 Sqn *Formidable* 1944, *Implacable* 1944
	829 Sqn *Victorious* 1944
	830 Sqn *Furious* 1943–44, *Formidable* 1944
	831 Sqn *Furious* 1944
	837 Sqn *Glory* 1945–46
	841 Sqn *Implacable* 1944
	847 Sqn *Illustrious* 1944
Grumman Avenger	820 Sqn *Indefatigable* 1945
	828 Sqn *Implacable* 1945–46
	832 Sqn *Victorious* 1943, *Illustrious* 1944, *Begum* 1944
	845 Sqn *Illustrious* 1944, *Ameer* 1944, *Empress* 1945, *Emperor* 1945
	846 Sqn *Tracker* 1944, *Trumpeter* 1944, 1945, *Premier* 1944
	848 Sqn *Formidable* 1945
	849 Sqn *Victorious* 1945
	851 Sqn *Shah* 1944–45
	852 Sqn *Nabob* 1944, *Trumpeter* 1944, *Fencer* 1944
	853 Sqn *Tracker* 1944, *Queen* 1945
	854 Sqn *Illustrious* 1944–45
	856 Sqn *Premier* 1944–45
	857 Sqn *Indomitable* 1944–45
	885 Sqn *Ruler* 1945
Vought Corsair	1830 Sqn *Illustrious* 1944--45
	1831 Sqn *Glory* 1945--46
	1833 Sqn *Illustrious* 1944–45
	1834 Sqn *Victorious* 1944–45
	1836 Sqn *Victorious* 1944–45
	1837 Sqn *Illustrious* 1944
	1838 Sqn *Victorious* 1944
	1841 Sqn *Formidable* 1944–45
	1842 Sqn *Formidable* 1944–45
	1846 Sqn *Colossus* 1945
	1850 Sqn *Vengeance* 1945–46
	1851 Sqn *Venerable* 1945–46
Grumman Hellcat	800 Sqn *Emperor* 1944–45
	804 Sqn *Emperor* 1944, *Ameer* 1945, *Empress* 1945
	804 Flt *Empress* 1945, *Shah* 1945
	808 Flt *Emperor* 1945
	808 Sqn *Khedive* 1945
	885 Sqn *Ruler* 1945
	888 Sqn *Indefatigable* 1945, *Empress* 1945, *Emperor* 1945, *Ameer* 1945
	896 Sqn *Ameer* 1945, *Empress* 1945
	1839 Sqn *Indomitable* 1944–45
	1840 Sqn *Furious* 1944, *Indefatigable* 1944, *Speaker* 1945
	1844 Sqn *Indomitable* 1944–45, *Formidable* 1945
	892 Sqn *Ocean* 1946
Fairey Firefly (Second World War)	1700 Sqn *Indefatigable* 1944–45
	1771 Sqn *Implacable* 1944–45
	1772 Sqn *Indefatigable* 1945
	1790 Sqn *Implacable* 1945–46
	1792 Sqn *Ocean* 1946
	746A Flt *Searcher* 1945
	882 Sqn *Vindex* 1945, *Searcher* 1945

Fairey Firefly (post-war)	810 Sqn *Theseus* 1949–51, *Ocean* 1953
	812 Sqn *Glory* 1951
	814 Sqn *Vengeance* 1950
	816 Sqn *Nairana* 1945, *Theseus* 1946, *Ocean* 1947
	821 Sqn *Glory* 1951–53
	825 Sqn *Ocean* 1952
	827 Sqn *Triumph* 1950
	837 Sqn *Glory* 1945–46
Blackburn Firebrand	813 Sqn *Illustrious* 1947–??, *Implacable* 1949–??, *Indomitable* 1952–53
	827 Sqn *Eagle* 1950–53
de Havilland Sea Hornet	801 Sqn *Implacable* 1949–51, *Indomitable* 1951
	809 Sqn *Vengeance* 1951, *Indomitable* 1952, *Eagle* 1952–54
Hawker Sea Fury	801 Sqn *Glory* 1951
	802 Sqn *Vengeance* 1949, *Ocean* 1950–52
	804 Sqn *Glory* 1950–52
	807 Sqn *Theseus* 1950–51, *Ocean* 1951–53
	811 Sqn *Warrior* 1953
Supermarine Attacker	800 Sqn *Eagle* 1952–54
	803 Sqn *Eagle* 1952–54
Douglas Skyraider	849 Sqn A Flt *Eagle* 1953–59; B Flt *Eagle* 1954, *Ark Royal* 1955–58, *Victorious* 1958–60; C Flt *Albion* 1954–59; D Flt *Albion* 1956, 1960, *Bulwark* 1957–58, *Centaur* 1959
Westland Wyvern	813 Sqn *Albion* 1954, *Eagle* 1955, 1957–58
	827 Sqn *Eagle* 1955
	830 Sqn *Eagle* 1956
	831 Sqn *Ark Royal* 1956–57
Hawker Sea Hawk	800 Sqn *Ark Royal* 1955, *Albion* 1956
	801 Sqn *Bulwark* 1958, *Centaur* 1959–60
	802 Sqn *Albion* 1956
	803 Sqn *Eagle* 1956
	804 Sqn *Eagle* 1955, 1957, *Ark Royal* 1956, *Bulwark* 1956, *Albion* 1958–59
	806 Sqn *Centaur* 1954, *Eagle* 1954, *Albion* 1959–60
	810 Sqn *Albion* 1955–56
	811 Sqn *Centaur*
	897 Sqn *Eagle* 1956, *Bulwark* 1956
	898 Sqn *Albion* 1954, *Ark Royal* 1955
	899 Sqn *Eagle* 1956
de Havilland Sea Venom	809 Sqn *Albion* 1956–59
	890 Sqn *Albion* 1955
	891 Sqn *Ark Royal* 1955–56, *Eagle* 1956, *Bulwark* 1957–58, *Centaur* 1959–60
	892 Sqn *Eagle* 1956–57
	893 Sqn *Eagle* 1956, *Ark Royal* 1957–58, *Victorious* 1958, 1959

Fairey Gannet

894 Sqn *Albion* 1956, 1960, *Eagle* 1957–59, *Victorious* 1959
895 Sqn *Albion* 1956
810 Sqn *Centaur* 1956
812 Sqn *Eagle* 1956
814 Sqn *Eagle* 1957
815 Sqn *Ark Royal* 1956–57
820 Sqn *Bulwark* 1957, *Centaur* 1958
824 Sqn *Ark Royal* 1955
825 Sqn *Albion* 1955
826 Sqn *Eagle* 1955
849 Sqn A Flt *Victorious* 1964–67, *Hermes* 1969; B Flt *Victorious* 1960–62, *Centaur* 1963, *Hermes* 1966–68, *Ark Royal* 1970–78; C Flt *Hermes* 1960–62, *Ark Royal* 1963–66; D Flt *Eagle* 1964–72

Supermarine Scimitar

800 Sqn *Ark Royal* 1961–63
800B Flt *Eagle* 1964–66
803 Sqn *Victorious* 1958–62, *Hermes* 1962, *Ark Royal* 1963–66
804 Sqn *Hermes* 19??
807 Sqn *Ark Royal* 1959–??

Westland Whirlwind

814 Sqn *Victorious* 1960
815 Sqn *Albion* 1958–60
820 Sqn *Albion* 1958
824 Sqn *Victorious* 1958, *Ark Royal* 1960, *Centaur* 1961–62
825 Sqn *Victorious* 1960–62
845 Sqn *Theseus* 1956

de Havilland Sea Vixen

890 Sqn *Hermes* 1960, *Ark Royal* 1963–66
892 Sqn *Ark Royal* 1960, *Victorious* 1960–62, *Centaur* 1963–66, *Hermes* 1966–68
893 Sqn *Victorious* 1960–67, *Hermes* 19??
899 Sqn *Eagle* 1965–72

Westland Wessex

814 Sqn *Hermes* 1962, *Victorious* 1963–67
815 Sqn *Ark Royal* 1961–66
819 Sqn *Ark Royal* 1965
820 Sqn *Eagle* 1967
826 Sqn *Hermes* 1966, *Eagle* 1969

Blackburn Buccaneer

800 Sqn *Eagle* 1964–65, 1967–72
801 Sqn *Ark Royal* 1963, *Victorious* 1963–64, 1966–67, *Hermes* 19??
809 Sqn *Hermes* 1967–68, *Ark Royal* 1970–78

McDonnell Phantom

892 Sqn *Ark Royal* 1970–78

Westland Sea King

814 Sqn *Hermes* 1973–77, *Bulwark* 1977–79, *Illustrious* 1982–
820 Sqn *Invincible* 1980–
824 Sqn *Ark Royal* 1970–78
824D Flt *Illustrious* 1982–
826 Sqn *Eagle* 1970–72, *Bulwark* 1979, *Hermes* 1981–

British Aerospace Sea Harrier

800 Sqn *Invincible* 1980, *Hermes* 1981–
801 Sqn *Invincible* 1981–
809 Sqn *Hermes* 1982, *Illustrious* 1982
899 Sqn *Hermes* and *Invincible* 1982

Select bibliography

Allward, Maurice, *Buccaneer*, Ian Allan, 1981.

Apps, Lieutenant-Commander Michael, *Send Her Victorious*, William Kimber, 1971; *The Four Ark Royals*, William Kimber, 1976.

Beaver, Paul, *Ark Royal*, Patrick Stephens, 1979; *The British Aircraft Carrier*, Patrick Stephens, 1982.

Bell Davies VC, Vice-Admiral Richard, *Sailor in the Air*, Peter Davies, 1967.

British Aviation Research Group, *A History of the Westland Wyvern*, 1973; *A History of the Douglas Skyraider AEW.1*, 1974.

Brown, David, *Carrier Air Groups: HMS Eagle*, Hylton Lacy, 1972; *Carrier Operations in World War II: Volume One The Royal Navy*, Ian Allan, revised edition 1974.

Brown, Captain Eric, *Wings on My Sleeve*, Airlife, 1978.

Friedman, Norman, *Carrier Air Power*, Conway Maritime Press, 1981.

Hanson, Norman, *Carrier Pilot*, Patrick Stephens, 1979.

Harrison, W. A., *Swordfish Special*, Ian Allan, 1977.

Johnson, Brian, *Fly Navy*, David & Charles, 1981.

Lord Kilbracken, *Bring Back My Stringbag*, Peter Davies, 1979, Pan Books, 1980.

Lamb, Commander Charles, *War in a Stringbag*, Cassell, 1977.

Lindsay, Roger, *de Havilland Venom*, 1973.

Longstaff, Reginald, *The Fleet Air Arm: A Pictorial History*, Robert Hale, 1981.

Milne, Lieutenant-Commander J. M., *Flashing Blades Over the Sea: the Development and History of Helicopters in the Royal Navy*, Maritime Books, 1981.

Poolman, Kenneth, *Ark Royal*, William Kimber, 1956, New English Library, 1974; *Escort Carrier 1941–1945,* Ian Allan, 1972.

Rawlings, John D. R., *Pictorial History of the Fleet Air Arm*, Ian Allan, 1973.

Roskill, Captain S. W., *Documents Relating to the Naval Air Service Volume One 1908–1918*, Navy Records Society, 1969.

Sturtivant, Ray, *Fleet Air Arm at War*, Ian Allan, 1982.

Thetford, Owen, *British Naval Aircraft since 1912*, Putnam, six editions 1958–82.

Till, Geoffrey, *Air Power and the Royal Navy 1914–1945*, Jane's, 1979.

Young, Desmond, *Rutland of Jutland*, Cassell, 1963.

Not to be forgotten are the many aviation and modelling periodicals which often contain articles on naval aviation which break new ground, for example Ray Sturtivant's twenty-page piece on 'Fleet Air Arm Colours 1923–33' in the March 1982 issue of *Scale Aircraft Modelling*.

Index

Aircraft are listed under name of manufacturer; ships are listed separately at the end.

Aden, 90, 95
Admiralty design category N.2a, 15, 19
Aegean Sea, 42, 44, 56
Aeroplane and Armament Experimental Establishment (A&AEE): Boscombe Down, 35, 40, 68, 71, 75, 84, 86, 89; Martlesham Heath, 17, 22, 27, 29, 30
Afrika Korps, 37
Agusta (helicopter manufacturer), 99
Aldermaston, 81
Alexandria, 35
Arbroath, 65
Arctic convoys, 42
Armstrong Whitworth: Sea Hawk production, 75
Atlantic convoys, 36, 42
Avro Bison, 18, 19

Baginton, 75
Baie de la Seine, 38
Beardmore (aircraft builder), 9, 11; WB III, 11
Bedford, Bill, 100
Belgium, 37
Belize, 95
Bergen, 33
Black, Flight Lieutenant A.M., 33
Blackburn: B-6, 29; Baffin, 17, 25, 30; Blackburn, 19; Buccaneer, 86, 93-95; Dart, 17, 19, 25; Firebrand, 62-64; GP, 14; Ripon, 17, 25; Roc, 34, 57; Shark, 25, 28-30; Skua, 26, 33-37; Swift, 17; Swordfish production, 32

Boulton Paul: Sea Fury design, 66
Boyce, Flight Lieutenant Gerald, 17
Bramwell, Lieutenant Commander H.P., 42
Brawdy, 78
Bristol (British & Colonial) (aircraft builder), 15; Scout C, 8; Type 173, 98; Type 192, 98
British Aerospace Sea Harrier, 78, 90, 99-102
Brooklands, 26
Brough, 29, 33, 62, 95, 96
Brown, Lieutenant Commander E.M., 45, 79
Brunswick, 51
Bumpus, Major F.A., 29

Camm, Sydney, 66
Cape Matapan, 37
Caudron GII, 7
Ceylon, 36
Chanak (Turkish crisis, 1922), 16
Chaplin, H.E., 57, 81
Chilbolton, 69
Christchurch, 89
Clyde, River, 38, 42, 56
Crete, 36, 37
Culdrose, 65, 70, 91, 98
Culley, Lieutenant Stuart, 13
Cunliffe-Owen: Seafire sub-contractor, 44

Dassault Mirage, 102
Davenport, Arthur, 71
de Havilland: DH 110, 89; DH 116, 89; Hornet, 64, 65; Sea Hornet, 64, 65; Sea Vampire, 79; Sea Venom,

79, 80, 89; Sea Vixen, 80, 89, 90, 96; Trident, 95; Vampire, 79; Venom, 80; de Havilland, Geoffrey, 64
Deck-landing: arrestor gear, 11, 16, 20, 22; early experiments, 10; on floats, 23; on Furious, 11, 12; undercarriage-less trials, 69, 80, 84
Dewoitine D 520, 44
Digby, John, 71
Dornier Do 18, 33
Douglas Skyraider, 70, 83
Dunning, Squadron Commander E.H., 11
Dunsfold, 101

EH Industries EH-101, 99
East Fortune, 14
Eastchurch, 6-8
Eglinton, 49, 53, 60, 66, 67
Egypt, 36, 40
Ely, Eugene, 6
Esmonde, Lieutenant Commander Eugene, 32

Fairey: III series early development, 19, 20; IIID, 15, 16, 19, 20, 22; IIIF, 18-20, 22, 23, 28; Albacore, 37, 38, 47, 49, 62; Barracuda, 38, 47-49, 51, 53; Firefly, 49, 57-62, 80; Flycatcher, 16, 20-22, 26, 27; Flycatcher II, 22; Fulmar, 34-36, 47, 57; Gannet, 51, 61, 70, 81-83, 88, 99; Seal, 23, 28, 30; Swordfish, 25, 28-32, 36, 37, 40, 42, 47, 49, 51, 62; TSR II, 30
Fairfield (aircraft builder), 14
Falklands conflict, 6, 83, 90, 99, 101, 102
Farley, John, 101
Fleet Air Arm units: 5th Naval Fighter Wing, 56; 7th Naval Fighter Wing,

56; 8th Torpedo-Bomber-Reconnaissance Wing, 47; 21st Torpedo-Bomber-Reconnaissance Wing, 49; 401 Flt, 16; 402 Flt, 22; 404 Flt, 26; 408 Flt, 27, 28; 409 Flt, 26, 28; 420 Flt, 18, 19; 421 Flt, 18; 422 Flt, 18, 19; 423 Flt, 18; 440 Flt, 16, 22; 441 Flt, 15, 20; 444 Flt, 20; 445 Flt, 20, 22; 446 Flt, 22; 447 Flt, 18; 448 Flt, 18; 449 Flt, 19; 450 Flt, 19; 460 Flt, 17; 461 Flt, 17, 25; 462 Flt, 17, 25; 700A Sqn, 101; 700B Sqn, 95; 700G Sqn, 83; 700H Sqn, 88, 91, 92; 700P Sqn, 96; 700S Sqn, 98; 700X Flt, 86; 700Y Sqn, 90; 700Z Sqn, 95; 703 Sqn, 65; 703W Flt, 73; 703X Flt, 81; 705 Sqn, 88; 706 Sqn, 88; 708 Sqn, 64; 737 Sqn, 92, 98; 767 Sqn, 97; 778 Sqn, 70; 800 Sqn, 28, 33, 34, 45, 47, 53, 56, 69, 86, 95, 101; 801 Sqn, 28, 33, 35, 40, 45, 65, 95; 802 Sqn, 28, 35, 39, 40, 61, 67, 78; 803 Sqn, 26, 33, 39, 69, 86, 95; 804 Sqn, 35, 36, 39, 40, 45, 47, 53; 805 Sqn, 36, 40; 806 Sqn, 36, 39, 78; 807 Sqn, 36, 42, 44, 45, 66, 67, 78; 808 Sqn, 36; 809 Sqn, 65, 80, 95; 810 Sqn, 17, 25, 29, 30, 31, 47, 49; 811 Sqn, 25, 30; 812 Sqn, 25, 30; 813 Sqn, 31, 35, 36, 40, 64, 73, 74; 814 Sqn, 60, 91, 92; 815 Sqn, 31, 49, 51, 91; 816 Sqn, 60; 817 Sqn, 60; 818 Sqn, 31; 819 Sqn, 31, 51, 91; 820 Sqn, 22, 23, 28-31, 38, 51, 88, 99; 821 Sqn, 28-30; 822 Sqn, 22, 28; 823 Sqn, 22; 824 Sqn, 22, 31, 40, 61, 81, 98, 99; 825 Sqn, 22, 28,

30-32, 60, 61; 826 Sqn, 37, 81, 98; 827 Sqn, 47, 61, 64, 73, 74; 829 Sqn, 37, 92; 830 Sqn, 47, 74; 831 Sqn, 74; 832 Sqn, 49, 51; 836 Sqn, 32; 845 Sqn, 88; 846 Sqn, 51; 847 Sqn, 49; 848 Sqn, 88; 849 Sqn, 70, 83; 880 Sqn, 39, 40, 44; 883 Sqn, 39; 885 Sqn, 44; 887 Sqn, 45; 889 Sqn, 44; 890 Sqn, 69, 80; 892 Sqn, 90, 97; 893 Sqn, 80; 894 Sqn, 45; 899 Sqn, 44, 90, 101; 1770 Sqn, 59; 1830 Sqn, 51, 53; 1833 Sqn, 53; 1834 Sqn, 53; 1839 Sqn, 56; 1840 Sqn, 56; 1841 Sqn, 53; 1844 Sqn, 56; Naval Air Fighting Development Unit, 65, 69; Service Trials Unit, 65
Focke Wulf: Fw 190, 42; Fw 200 Condor, 39, 40
Folland, H.P., 15
Ford, 37, 64, 65, 69, 73, 74, 81, 86
Formosa, 56
Fowler, Flight Lieutenant, 8
France, 40
Freetown, 33

Garner, Squadron Leader Peter, 71
Gibraltar convoys, 36, 40, 56
Gloster: Gladiator, 34; Javelin, 89; Meteor, 74; Sea Gladiator, 28, 34, 35, 57
Gloucestershire Mars X, 15
Gosport, 14, 17-19, 29
Grain (Isle of), Experimental Construction Depot, Port Victoria, 10, 14
Grain Griffin, 14
Graves, Squadron Leader Mike, 73
Gray, Lieutenant Robert Hampton, 53
Greece, 40
Grimsetter, 59
Grumman: Avenger, 38, 42, 49-51, 61, 70; Hellcat, 50, 53-56, 60; Martlet/Wildcat, 36, 40-42, 53

Hamble, 22
Handley Page Harrow, 25
Harmondsworth, 30
Hatfield, 65
Hatston, 33, 40, 59
Hawker: Fury (i), 27; Fury (ii), 66; Hart, 26, 35;

Hoopoe, 27; Hurricane, 39; Nimrod, 22, 26-28, 34; Osprey, 22, 26; P.1040, 75; P.1127, 96, 100; P.1154, 96, 100; Sea Fury, 61, 66-68; Sea Hawk, 67, 74-78; Sea Hurricane, 38-40; Tempest, 66; Typhoon, 62
Hawker, Harry, 9
Hawker Siddeley Harrier, 100, 101
Hayes, 57
Heathrow (Great West Aerodrome), 57
Heligoland Bight, 13
Heston, 65
Heston Aircraft: Sea Hornet design, 64, 65
Hollis Williams, D.L., 81
Hucclecote, 34
Humble, Bill, 75

Indian Ocean, 35, 42, 44, 51, 56, 60
Indonesian confrontation, 95

Japan, 45, 49, 51
Java, 51
Junkers Ju 88, 40

Kingston, 66, 75, 100
Kirkenes, 37, 39
Korean War, 47, 61, 67

Leconfield, 62
Lee-on-Solent, 36, 37, 42, 64, 65, 81
Leuchars, 15, 20, 22
Lithgow, Lieutenant Commander Michael, 69, 84, 86
Lobelle, Marcel, 30
London, 64
Lossiemouth, 86, 95

McClean, Francis, 6
McDonnell Phantom, 95-97, 100
Macfarlane, Lieutenant B.D., 73
Machrihanish, 62
Macmillan, Norman, 22
Malaya, 47, 48
Malone, Lieutenant C.L'Estrange, 7
Malta, 35, 40, 80
Manston, 32
Marine Aircraft Experimental Establishment (MAEE), Felixstowe, 26, 27
Mason, Roy, 101

Mediterranean Sea, 31, 35-37, 39, 40, 42, 74
Medway, River, 6
MiG-15, 67, 80
Mitchell, Reginald, 16, 68
Mutual Defense Assistance Program, 51, 61, 70, 88

Narvik, 31, 33, 38
Naval manoeuvres (1913), 7
Netherlands, 60
Nicholl, Colonel Vincent, 20, 22
Nieuport: Nighthawk, 15; Nightjar, 15, 16
North Africa, 37
North Cape, 36
Norfolk, Virginia, 49, 50
Norway (coastal operations), 35, 38, 40, 44, 47, 51, 56, 60

Operations: Avalanche (Salerno landings), 44; Corporate (Falklands repossession), 90; Dragoon (South of France), 44; Goodwood (*Tirpitz* attacks), 56; Harpoon (Malta convoy), 40; Husky (Sicily invasion), 44; Mascot (*Tirpitz* attacks), 56, 59; Musketeer (Suez campaign), 70; Pedestal (Malta convoy), 40; Torch (North African landings), 38, 40, 42; Tungsten (*Tirpitz* attacks), 47, 53, 56

Pacific Ocean (theatre of war), 49, 51, 56, 60, 64, 65, 70
Parnall: Panther, 15, 20; Plover, 20
Patuxent River, 60
Penrose, Harald, 71
Petsamo, 37, 39
Petter, W.E.W., 71
Petty, G.E., 33, 62
Port Victoria—*see* Grain
Portland, 98
Portsmouth, 74

Quill, Jeffrey, 68
Quonset, 50, 51

Radar: AI Mk X, 59; AN/APS-6, 56; APS-20, 70; ASH, 49, 59, 65; ASV, 32, 81, 91; ASV Mk IIN, 49; ASV Mk X, 49; airborne early warning, 70, 83, 99; Blue Fox, 101; Sea

Searcher, 99; Searchwater, 99
Ringway airport, Manchester, 35
Royal Aero Club, 6
RAF Coastal Command, 37, 49
RAF units: 3 Sqn, 18; 9 Sqn, 59; 46 Sqn, 38; 185 Sqn, 14; 203 Sqn, 16; 205 Sqn, 15; 617 Sqn, 59; Merchant Ship Fighter Unit, 39
Royal Aircraft Establishment (RAE): Bedford, 86, 89, 95, 97; Farnborough, 66, 80
Royal Canadian Air Force unit: 415 Sqn, 38
Royal Canadian Navy, 60
Royal Flying Corps, Naval Wing, 7
Royal Navy formations and stations: 11th Aircraft Carrier Squadron, 49; China Station, 19, 20, 26; Eastern Fleet, 45; Harwich Force, 13; Home Fleet, 17, 39; Mediterranean Fleet, 17, 19, 20
Rutland, Flight Commander F.J., 9-11

Sabang, 49, 53
St Louis, 96
Sakishima Gunto, 56
Salerno, 38
Samson, Colonel Charles Rumney, 6, 7, 13
Scapa Flow, 11, 35
Scottish Aviation: Avenger conversion, 51; Wildcat re-erection, 40
Sembawang, 47
Short: biplanes, 6; modified S 38, 6
Sicily, 38
Sikorsky helicopters: S-51, 86; S-55, 88; S-58, 91; S-61, 98
Singapore, 95
Slade, Group Captain R. Gordon, 81
Slattery, Rear Admiral Sir Matthew, 71
Smart, Flight Sub-Lieutenant B.A., 9
Smith, Joseph, 68
Solomon Islands, 42, 45, 51
Sopwith: 1½-strutter, 11, 12; 2F.1 Camel, 12, 13, 16; B-1, 14; Baby, 9; Cuckoo, 14, 17; Pup, 9-11; Schneider, 8
South Atlantic, 33

Specifications: 6/22, 20; 38/22, 20; 21/23, 25; N.21/26, 27; O.22/26, 26; 16/30, 27; 4/33, 25; S.15/33, 29, 30; P.4/34, 35; O.27/34, 33; S.38/34, 30; S.41/36, 37; S.24/37, 47; O.8/38, 35; N.8/39, 57; N.9/39, 57; N.5/40, 57; N.11/40, 62; F.1/43, 68; F.2/43, 66; N.4/43, 45; N.7/43, 66; S.8/43, 62; F.12/43, 64; N.22/43, 66; N.5/44, 64; N.7/44, 45; E.10/44, 68; N.11/44, 71; E.1/45, 68; N.12/45, 71; GR.17/45, 81; N.21/45, 65; N.7/46, 75; N.9/47, 84; T.12/48, 73; N.107, 80; N.113D, 86; N.113P, 86; M.148T, 93; AEW.154P, 83
Squantum, 50
Staniland, C.S., 28, 30, 35, 57
Stretton, 47
Sueter, Commodore Murray, 14
Suez Canal, 36, 74, 78, 80
Sumatra, 51, 53, 56
Supermarine: 392 Jet Spiteful, 68; 505, 84; 508, 84; 525, 84, 86; 529, 84; Attacker, 68, 69, 84; Scimitar, 84-86; Sea Lion II, 16; Sea Otter, 16; Seafire, 36, 40, 42-47, 66; Seagull II, 16; Seal, 16; Spiteful, 68; Spitfire, 42, 45, 68; Swift, 84

Taranto, 31, 35
Thompson, Flight Lieutenant Arthur, 62
Tokyo, 51, 60
Tondern, 12

Torpedo Aeroplane School, East Fortune, 14

United States Navy: 3rd Fleet, 45

Vought Corsair, 51-53

Watson, Bernard, 95
Welsh, Flight Lieutenant W.L., 8
West Raynham, 69
Westland: Dragonfly, 88; Sea King, 98, 99; Seafire production, 44; WG 1, 98; Wasp, 92; Wessex, 91, 92, 98; Whirlwind, 81, 86-88, 91, 98; Wyvern, 64, 71-74
Weymouth Bay, 7
Whitehead, Lieutenant Commander Derek, 95
Woodward, Rear Admiral John, 101
Worthy Down, 33, 36

Yeovil, 86, 98
Yeovilton, 59, 60, 80, 90, 96, 101

Zeppelin airships: L.23, 9; L.53, 13; L.54, 12; L.60, 12

Index of ships
United Kingdom

Activity, 51; Africa, 6; Albion, 70, 73, 78, 80, 89; Argus, 12-16, 18-20, 22, 36, 42, 44; Ariguani, 36; Ark Royal (I), 26, 31, 33, 36; Ark Royal (II), 74, 83, 86, 89-91, 95, 97, 98, 100; Atheling, 44; Attacker, 44; Audacity, 40; Avenger, 32, 39
Battler, 44; Beagle, 51; Ben-my-Chree, 8; Biter, 44; Blake, 98; Bulwark, 78, 98
Campania (I), 8; Campania (II), 36; Catapult armed merchant ships (CAM-Ships), 39; Centaur, 83, 89; Colossus, 49; Courageous, 17, 20, 22, 26, 28, 29, 35
Devonshire, 92
Eagle (I), 13, 16-19, 22, 27, 31, 35, 40; Eagle (II), 65, 69, 70, 74, 75, 78, 80, 81, 84, 86, 90, 95, 97, 98, 100; Emperor, 56
Formidable, 37, 38, 42, 44, 53; Furious, 10, 11, 12, 17, 18, 22, 23, 28, 33, 35, 37, 39, 42, 44, 47, 56
Glorious, 22, 25-28, 35, 38; Glory, 45, 49
Hermes (I), 7; Hermes (II), 15, 18, 20, 26; Hermes (III), 83, 98, 101; Hibernia, 7; Hood, 22; Hunter, 44, 45
Illustrious (I), 31, 35, 36, 42, 47, 49, 51, 53, 59, 62, 64-66, 69, 71, 73, 75, 80, 81; Illustrious (II), 99; Implacable, 44, 45, 60, 65, 71; Indefatigable, 44, 45, 51, 56, 59, 60; Indomitable, 40, 44, 45, 56, 65; Invincible, 99, 101, 102
London, 7
Magnificent, 60; Manxman, 9; Maplin, 39; Merchant aircraft carriers (MAC-Ships), 32
Ocean, 45, 47, 61, 65, 66, 79
Pegasus, 36; Perseus, 88
Ravager, 56; Redoubt, 13; Repulse, 10
Sheffield (I), 32; Sheffield (II), 99; Speaker, 56; Springbank, 36; Stalker, 44, 45; Striker, 40
Terrible, 60; Theseus, 45, 67; Tiger, 98; Tracker, 51; Triumph, 45, 47, 61
Unicorn, 44
Venerable, 45, 49, 60; Vengeance, 49, 65, 67; Victorious, 31, 37, 40, 42, 47, 49, 51, 53, 66, 80, 83, 86, 90, 95; Vindex, 8, 12; Vindictive, 14, 20
Warrior, 60, 80; Warspite, 31
Yarmouth, 9

Australia

Australia, 12; Sydney, 60

France

Béarn, 40

Germany

Bismarck, 31, 32; Gneisenau, 32, 35, 38; Greif, 38; Königsberg, 33; midget submarines, 49; Prinz Eugen, 32; Scharnhorst, 32, 35, 38; Tirpitz, 37, 47, 53, 56, 59; U64, 31; U73, 40; U198, 51; U288, 51; U355, 51; U751, 40

Italy

Vittorio Veneto, 37

Japan

Amakusa, 53

Netherlands

Karel Doorman, 60

Soviet Union

Sverdlov class, 93

Spain

Dédalo, 100

United States

Birmingham, 6; Charger, 50; Pennsylvania, 6; Saratoga (I), 49; Saratoga (II), 97

Merchant ships

Ohio, tanker, 40; Torrey Canyon, tanker, 95

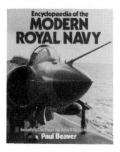